Bali Travel Guide

BnW Travel Series

Ashok Kumawat

Disclaimer: The information provided in this Bali travel guide is intended for general guidance and educational purposes only. While every effort has been made to ensure the accuracy and reliability of the information, we cannot guarantee its completeness or timeliness. Travel conditions, attractions, and services in Bali may change, and it is recommended to verify the latest details with official sources before making any travel arrangements. The author and publisher of this guide shall not be held responsible for any loss, injury, or inconvenience arising from the use of the information provided. Travelers are advised to exercise caution, follow local laws and customs, and make informed decisions based on their own research and personal circumstances.

Tale of contents:

Introduction to Bali: An Island Paradise

Welcome to Bali, the Island of the Gods - an enchanting destination that captivates travelers with its mystical allure, natural beauty, and rich cultural heritage. Located in the Indonesian archipelago, Bali is a tropical paradise known for its lush landscapes, stunning beaches, ancient temples, vibrant festivals, and warm-hearted locals. This introductory chapter sets the stage for your journey through this extraordinary island as we delve into its unique charm and unveil the wonders that await you.

Geographically, Bali is nestled between the islands of Java and Lombok, with the Bali Sea to the north and the Indian Ocean to the south. This strategic location gives the island a diverse range of landscapes, from towering volcanoes and terraced rice fields to serene beaches and lush rainforests. The tropical climate of Bali ensures that the island remains a year-round destination, welcoming travelers seeking sun, adventure, and cultural experiences in equal measure.

For centuries, Bali has been a melting pot of different cultures and civilizations, which is evident in its arts, traditions, and religious practices. The Balinese people are deeply rooted in their beliefs, predominantly following Hinduism, and their spirituality is an integral part of their daily lives. Balinese Hinduism is a unique blend of Indian Hinduism and indigenous beliefs, resulting in an intriguing tapestry of rituals and ceremonies that color the island with a sense of sacredness.

The island's spiritual essence is palpable in the numerous temples that grace its landscape. Bali is adorned with thousands of temples, ranging from humble village shrines to majestic sea temples, each offering an insight into the island's religious fabric. Some of the must-visit temples include the iconic Uluwatu Temple perched on a cliff, Tanah Lot Temple surrounded by the sea, and Besakih Temple, often referred to as the "Mother Temple of Bali."

Beyond its religious heritage, Bali is equally renowned for its arts and crafts, which are an integral part of the island's cultural identity. Artistic expressions like traditional dance, music, painting, and woodcarving are preserved through generations, showcasing Bali's innate creativity. Ubud, the cultural heart of Bali, is a hub for artists and artisans, where you can witness master craftsmen at work and bring home authentic Balinese souvenirs.

For nature enthusiasts, Bali offers a plethora of breathtaking landscapes and outdoor activities. From surfing the world-class breaks of Uluwatu and Canggu to trekking through the emerald-green rice terraces of Tegalalang, Bali provides an array of adventures that cater to different interests and skill levels. Scuba divers and snorkelers will be enthralled by the underwater wonders found off Bali's coast, where vibrant coral reefs and diverse marine life await exploration.

Bali's coastal regions offer an array of stunning beaches that cater to sun seekers, water sports enthusiasts, and those simply seeking relaxation. Seminyak, Kuta, and Nusa Dua are well-known for their lively beach scenes, while the quieter shores of Jimbaran and Sanur provide a more tranquil atmosphere for leisurely strolls and rejuvenating sunsets.

Cultural immersion is a quintessential part of the Balinese experience, and the island's festivals and celebrations are a testament to this. Witnessing a traditional temple festival or joining the vivacious processions during Galungan and Nyepi, the Day of Silence, provides a deeper understanding of the island's rich cultural tapestry.

As you embark on your journey to Bali, it's essential to respect and embrace the local customs and traditions. Balinese culture places a strong emphasis on community, family values, and harmony with nature. Simple gestures like wearing a sarong when visiting temples and participating in traditional customs with genuine respect will be warmly appreciated by the Balinese people.

This book will serve as your comprehensive guide to exploring Bali, ensuring that you make the most of your time on this enchanting island. We will provide you with insider tips, detailed itineraries, and recommendations to help you navigate Bali's diverse attractions, choose the best accommodations, savor the local cuisine, and make lasting memories.

Get ready to embark on a journey that will awaken your senses, nourish your soul, and leave you with a profound appreciation for the beauty and magic of Bali. Let the adventure begin!

Essential Travel Tips for Bali

Traveling to Bali, the Island of the Gods, is a dream come true for many. With its stunning landscapes, rich cultural heritage, and warm hospitality, Bali has become a favorite destination for travelers from around the world. To make your trip to this tropical paradise smooth, enjoyable, and hassle-free, we have compiled a comprehensive list of essential travel tips. From packing wisely to respecting local customs, these tips will help you make the most of your Bali experience.

Visa and Passport Requirements:

Before traveling to Bali, ensure that your passport is valid for at least six months from your date of entry. Most nationalities can enter Indonesia visa-free for up to 30 days, while some countries may require a visa on arrival or an e-visa. Check the visa requirements for your specific country before you depart.

Best Time to Visit:

Bali's tropical climate means it can be visited year-round, but the best time to travel is during the dry season from April to October. This period offers pleasant weather with lower humidity and less rainfall, making it ideal for outdoor activities and sightseeing.

Packing Essentials:

Pack light, comfortable clothing suitable for the tropical climate. Don't forget to bring swimwear, sunscreen, a hat, sunglasses, insect repellent, and a reusable water bottle. Bali is relatively casual, so there's no need for formal attire, unless you plan to visit high-end restaurants or attend specific events.

Respect Local Customs:

Bali's culture is deeply rooted in Hinduism, and it's essential to respect local customs and traditions. When visiting temples, wear a sarong and sash (often provided at the entrance) as a sign of respect. Avoid pointing with your feet, as they are considered impure, and refrain from public displays of affection, especially in religious areas.

Learning Basic Phrases:

Learning a few basic phrases in Bahasa Indonesia, the local language, can go a long way in connecting with the locals and showing appreciation for their culture. Simple greetings like "Selamat pagi" (good morning), "Terima kasih" (thank you), and "Permisi" (excuse me) are always well-received.

Transportation in Bali:

Bali offers various transportation options, including taxis, ride-hailing services, and motorbike rentals. Stick to reputable taxi companies or use ride-hailing apps to avoid scams. If you plan to rent a motorbike, ensure you have a valid international driver's license and wear a helmet at all times.

Traffic and Driving:

Bali's traffic can be hectic, especially in touristy areas like Kuta and Seminyak. Plan your activities accordingly and allow extra time for traveling. Be cautious when crossing the streets and use pedestrian crossings whenever possible.

Money Matters:

The local currency in Bali is the Indonesian Rupiah (IDR). ATMs are widely available in tourist areas, but it's a good idea to carry some cash, especially for small purchases and in case of emergencies. Inform your bank about your travel dates to avoid any issues with your cards.

Bargaining at Markets:

Bargaining is a common practice in Bali's markets and street stalls. When haggling, do so with a smile and maintain a friendly attitude. Remember that the goal is to reach a fair price that both you and the seller are happy with.

Drinking Water:

It's advisable to drink bottled or filtered water during your stay in Bali. Refrain from drinking tap water, and be cautious with ice in drinks, as it may be made from tap water.

Health and Safety Precautions:

Ensure you have travel insurance that covers medical expenses and emergencies. Protect yourself from mosquito bites by using insect repellent and wearing long sleeves and pants, especially during dawn and dusk. Apply sunscreen regularly to protect your skin from the strong tropical sun.

Balinese Cuisine:

Indulge in the flavors of Balinese cuisine, which is known for its rich spices and diverse influences. Be adventurous and try local dishes such as nasi goreng (fried rice), satay (grilled skewered meat), and babi guling (suckling pig). However, be cautious when consuming street food and ensure it's prepared hygienically.

Exploring Beyond the Tourist Areas:

While Bali's popular tourist areas are undoubtedly captivating, consider venturing off the beaten path to discover the island's hidden gems. Explore charming villages, hike through rice terraces, or visit lesser-known temples to experience the authentic side of Bali.

Environmental Responsibility:

Bali is known for its natural beauty, and it's important to practice responsible tourism to preserve its fragile ecosystems. Dispose of waste properly, reduce the use of single-use plastics, and support eco-friendly initiatives.

Embrace the Balinese Lifestyle:

Immerse yourself in the warmth and hospitality of the Balinese people. Engage in conversations, attend local ceremonies, and participate in cultural activities to gain a deeper appreciation for Bali's unique way of life.

By keeping these essential travel tips in mind, you'll be well-prepared to embark on an unforgettable journey through Bali. Get ready to soak up the sun, explore ancient temples, indulge in delicious cuisine, and create lifelong memories on this island paradise.

Best Time to Visit Bali: Weather and Seasons

Bali, the picturesque island paradise in Indonesia, offers a tropical climate that welcomes travelers throughout the year. However, understanding the weather patterns and the distinct seasons can greatly enhance your Bali experience. In this chapter, we will delve into the best time to visit Bali, providing you with valuable insights into the island's weather, seasons, and the activities each season offers.

Bali experiences two primary seasons: the dry season and the wet season. Let's explore these seasons in more detail.

Dry Season (April to October):

The dry season in Bali, also known as the high season, is the most popular time for tourists to visit the island. Spanning from April to October, this period offers pleasant weather characterized by warm temperatures, low humidity, and minimal rainfall. These conditions create ideal conditions for outdoor activities, sightseeing, and beach exploration.

The months of April, May, June, and September are particularly favorable for traveling to Bali. During these months, you can expect warm and sunny days with comfortable temperatures ranging from 26 to 30 degrees Celsius (79 to 86 degrees Fahrenheit). It's an excellent time for water sports, such as surfing, snorkeling, and diving, as the seas are calm and visibility is excellent.

July and August are peak months in Bali,

attracting a large influx of tourists. While the weather remains fantastic during this period, the popular tourist areas can be crowded. Planning your itinerary in advance and booking accommodations and activities early can help ensure a smooth and enjoyable trip.

Wet Season (November to March):

The wet season in Bali spans from November to March, characterized by higher humidity, occasional rainfall, and lush, green landscapes. Despite being the rainy season, Bali's tropical showers are typically short-lived and interspersed with periods of sunshine.

November and December mark the transitional period between the dry and wet seasons. The weather is generally pleasant, with sporadic rainfall that doesn't significantly hinder outdoor activities. However, it's advisable to pack a light rain jacket or umbrella for occasional showers.

From January to March, the rainfall increases, and the wet season is in full swing. Although it's the rainiest time in Bali, the island still offers plenty of charms and activities to enjoy. The rain showers often occur in the late afternoon or evening, leaving the mornings relatively dry for exploration and adventure. Plus, the island's lush greenery and rice terraces are at their most vibrant during this time.

It's worth noting that despite being the wet season, Bali continues to receive visitors. The island's popular cultural events and festivals, such as Galungan and Nyepi, take place during this time, offering unique cultural experiences.

Choosing the best time to visit Bali depends on your preferences and the activities you wish to engage in. If you prefer sunny and dry weather, the dry season is the ideal time for you. However, if you don't mind occasional showers and would like to experience Bali's lush landscapes and cultural events, the wet season can be just as rewarding.

It's important to keep in mind that weather patterns can vary from year to year, and unexpected weather conditions can occur. Therefore, it's always advisable to check the weather forecast closer to your travel dates and pack accordingly.

In terms of crowds and pricing, the dry season tends to be busier, with higher hotel rates and more tourists. If you prefer a more relaxed and budget-friendly experience, consider visiting during the shoulder months of April, May, June, or September.

Overall, Bali's tropical climate ensures that it remains an inviting destination year-round. Whether you visit during the dry season or the wet season, Bali's natural beauty, vibrant culture, and warm hospitality will leave you with cherished memories and a desire to return to this enchanting island time and time again.

Getting to Bali: Transportation Options

Bali, the Island of the Gods, is a highly sought-after destination that welcomes travelers from all corners of the globe. Situated in the Indonesian archipelago, Bali is well-connected to major international hubs, making it easily accessible for visitors. In this chapter, we will explore the various transportation options available to reach Bali, helping you plan your journey smoothly and efficiently.

By Air:

Ngurah Rai International Airport, also known as Denpasar International Airport (DPS), is the main gateway to Bali. It is located in the southern part of the island, near the capital city of Denpasar. The airport serves numerous international airlines and offers direct flights from major cities around the world, including Singapore, Kuala Lumpur, Hong Kong, Sydney, and Tokyo, among others.

From the airport, you can easily reach your accommodation by taking a taxi or arranging a transfer service. Taxis are available at the designated taxi counters outside the airport terminal, and reputable ride-hailing apps are also commonly used in Bali.

Connecting Flights:

If there are no direct flights from your location to Bali, you can opt for connecting flights through major Southeast Asian cities such as Singapore, Kuala Lumpur, or Jakarta. Several airlines offer convenient connecting flights to Bali, allowing you to plan your journey based on your preferred airlines and schedules.

Domestic Flights:

If you are already in Indonesia, domestic flights are a convenient option to reach Bali. The country has numerous airlines that operate regular flights to Bali from various cities, including Jakarta, Surabaya, Yogyakarta, and Lombok, among others. Flight durations are relatively short, making it an efficient way to travel within the country.

Ferry from Other Indonesian Islands:

Bali is well-connected to neighboring islands through ferry services. If you are exploring other parts of Indonesia, such as Java or Lombok, you can take a ferry to Bali. The most common ferry routes to Bali are from Java's ports, including Banyuwangi and Gilimanuk. Ferry services are available for both passengers and vehicles, providing an alternative transportation option with scenic views of the ocean.

Cruise Ships:

Bali is a popular destination for cruise ships sailing through Southeast Asia. Some luxury cruise lines include Bali as part of their itineraries, allowing passengers to experience the island's beauty and cultural highlights. Bali has several ports that accommodate cruise ships, such as Benoa Port and Padang Bai Port.

Overland Travel:

For travelers already in Indonesia or Southeast

Asia, overland travel to Bali can be an adventurous option. It involves taking buses, trains, or private cars to reach the island. However, overland travel to Bali requires careful planning and consideration of travel time, as it can be time-consuming and involve multiple transfers.

Visa Requirements:

Before traveling to Bali, ensure that you have checked the visa requirements for your specific nationality. Most nationalities can enter Indonesia visa-free for up to 30 days, while others require a visa on arrival or an e-visa. Make sure your passport has a validity of at least six months from your date of entry.

Transportation within Bali:

Once you have arrived in Bali, there are several transportation options available for getting around the island. Taxis are readily available, especially in tourist areas, and you can use reputable ride-hailing apps for convenience. Motorbike rentals are also popular, providing a flexible and affordable way to explore the island. However, ensure that you have a valid international driver's license and wear a helmet at all times.

Additionally, private drivers and tour operators offer services for day trips and customized itineraries, allowing you to explore Bali at your own pace. Public buses and minibusses, known as "bemos," are available but may not be as convenient for tourists, as they have fixed routes and schedules.

When planning your transportation in Bali, consider factors such as your budget, itinerary, and personal preferences. Each option has its advantages, so choose the one that suits your needs best and ensures a comfortable and enjoyable journey to the island of Bali.

With a range of transportation options and easy accessibility, reaching Bali has never been more convenient. Prepare for an unforgettable experience as you set foot on the shores of this breathtaking island.

Top Attractions in Bali

Bali, with its diverse landscapes, rich culture, and stunning natural beauty, offers an array of attractions that cater to every traveler's interests. From pristine beaches and lush rice terraces to ancient temples and vibrant markets, the island is a treasure trove of unforgettable experiences. In this chapter, we will explore some of the top attractions in Bali, ensuring that you don't miss out on the must-see highlights during your visit.

Ubud:

Known as the cultural heart of Bali, Ubud is a charming town nestled among lush greenery and terraced rice fields. Explore the famous Monkey Forest Sanctuary, visit the iconic Ubud Royal Palace, and immerse yourself in traditional Balinese art and craft at the numerous galleries and workshops. Don't miss the vibrant Ubud Market, where you can shop for local handicrafts, textiles, and souvenirs.

Tanah Lot Temple:

Perched on a rocky outcrop overlooking the Indian Ocean, Tanah Lot Temple is one of Bali's most iconic landmarks. The temple is particularly renowned for its dramatic sunset views. Take in the enchanting scenery, explore the temple's intricately carved shrines, and witness traditional Balinese ceremonies that often take place here.

Uluwatu Temple:

Located atop a cliff on the Bukit Peninsula, Uluwatu Temple offers breathtaking panoramic views of the Indian Ocean. This ancient sea temple is known for its stunning architecture and captivating Balinese Kecak dance performances that take place against the backdrop of the setting sun. Be mindful of the mischievous resident monkeys and dress modestly when visiting this sacred site.

Kuta Beach:

For those seeking sun, sand, and surf, Kuta Beach is a must-visit destination. This bustling beach is famous for its vibrant atmosphere, ideal waves for beginner surfers, and an array of beachside bars and restaurants. Enjoy the laid-back beach vibes, take surf lessons, or simply relax and soak up the sun.

Tegalalang Rice Terraces:

A visit to Bali wouldn't be complete without witnessing the awe-inspiring Tegalalang Rice Terraces near Ubud. These iconic terraces showcase Bali's agricultural heritage and offer breathtaking views of the sculpted rice paddies. Take a leisurely stroll through the terraces, interact with local farmers, and capture stunning photographs of this natural masterpiece.

Mount Batur:

Adventure enthusiasts shouldn't miss the opportunity to climb Mount Batur, an active volcano located in the northeastern part of Bali. Trek to the summit before dawn and be rewarded with a majestic sunrise over the surrounding landscape, including Lake Batur. The hike is challenging but manageable for most fitness levels, and the experience is truly unforgettable.

Nusa Penida:

Escape the crowds and explore the natural wonders of Nusa Penida, a neighboring island of Bali. Marvel at the stunning cliffs of Kelingking Beach, swim in the crystal-clear waters of Angel's Billabong, and snorkel alongside manta rays at Manta Point. Nusa Penida offers a tranquil retreat and an opportunity to connect with Bali's raw and untouched beauty.

Tirta Empul Temple:

Experience a spiritual cleansing ritual at Tirta Empul Temple, a sacred water temple located in the village of Tampaksiring. The temple features a series of holy spring pools, where visitors can participate in a traditional purification ritual. This unique cultural experience offers insight into Bali's spiritual beliefs and practices.

Seminyak:

Indulge in the chic and trendy atmosphere of Seminyak, a vibrant coastal town known for its upscale resorts, designer boutiques, and world-class restaurants. Enjoy a day of pampering at luxurious spas, explore the fashionable Seminyak Square, and savor delectable cuisine at the hip beach clubs along the Seminyak coastline.

Goa Gajah:

Also known as the Elephant Cave, Goa Gajah is an ancient archaeological site located near Ubud. Explore the intricate carvings and hidden chambers of this mysterious cave, which dates back to the 11th century. Admire the bathing pools, statues, and tranquil surroundings that make Goa Gajah a unique cultural and historical attraction.

These are just a few of the top attractions that Bali has to offer. The island is filled with countless more temples, waterfalls, traditional villages, and natural wonders waiting to be discovered. Whether you seek adventure, relaxation, or cultural immersion, Bali's attractions will leave you awe-inspired and longing to return to this captivating island paradise.

Exploring Bali's Stunning Beaches

Bali, with its miles of pristine coastline and turquoise waters, is a tropical paradise renowned for its stunning beaches. Whether you're a sun seeker, a water sports enthusiast, or simply looking to unwind and relax, Bali's beaches offer something for everyone. In this chapter, we will explore some of the most breathtaking beaches in Bali, ensuring that you experience the best of what the island has to offer.

Kuta Beach:

Kuta Beach is one of Bali's most famous and vibrant beaches. Located on the southwestern coast of the island, it offers a lively atmosphere with a wide range of activities. Surfing is particularly popular here, thanks to the consistent waves that are suitable for both beginners and experienced surfers. Rent a board and catch some waves or simply relax on the golden sand, enjoying the energetic vibe of Kuta.

Seminyak Beach:

Adjacent to Kuta, Seminyak Beach offers a more upscale and sophisticated atmosphere. It's a haven for luxury resorts, high-end beach clubs, and trendy restaurants. Enjoy a leisurely day sunbathing on the soft sand, treat yourself to a spa session, or indulge in a delectable meal at one of the beachfront establishments. Seminyak Beach is also known for its stunning sunsets, so make sure to find a cozy spot and witness the sky ablaze with hues of orange and pink.

Nusa Dua Beach:

Situated on Bali's southeastern coast, Nusa Dua Beach is known for its crystal-clear waters and tranquil surroundings. The beach is part of a gated resort area that offers a serene and luxurious experience. Enjoy swimming, snorkeling, or diving in the calm waters, which are protected by offshore reefs. Nusa Dua Beach is also home to several high-end resorts and golf courses, providing a perfect combination of relaxation and leisure activities.

Padang Padang Beach:

Nestled between towering cliffs on the Bukit Peninsula, Padang Padang Beach is a hidden gem that offers breathtaking beauty. Accessible through a narrow rock crevice, the beach welcomes visitors to its secluded shores and turquoise waters. It's a favorite spot for surfers, as the waves here can be quite challenging but rewarding. Enjoy the laid-back atmosphere, soak up the sun, and take in the dramatic scenery surrounding this picturesque beach.

Jimbaran Beach:

Located in the fishing village of Jimbaran, this beach is famous for its idyllic setting and fresh seafood dining experiences. Picture soft sand, swaying palm trees, and traditional fishing boats lining the shore. In the evening, the beach comes alive with candlelit seafood barbecues, where you can savor a variety of freshly caught seafood while enjoying a romantic sunset view.

Balangan Beach:

For those seeking a more secluded and tranquil beach experience, Balangan Beach is a hidden gem worth exploring. This pristine stretch of white sand is backed by cliffs and offers breathtaking panoramic views. The beach is known for its consistent waves, making it a favorite spot for experienced surfers. If you're not into surfing, you can still enjoy the serene ambiance, take a leisurely walk along the shore, or simply bask in the beauty of this untouched paradise.

Dreamland Beach:

Dreamland Beach, also known as New Kuta Beach, is another beautiful beach located on the Bukit Peninsula. It's a popular destination for sunbathing, swimming, and surfing. The beach is surrounded by dramatic cliffs and offers a relaxed and less crowded atmosphere compared to some of the busier tourist areas. Enjoy the picturesque setting, indulge in water sports activities, or simply unwind on the soft sand.

Amed Beach:

Located on Bali's east coast, Amed Beach offers a completely different beach experience compared to the popular tourist areas. It's a peaceful and laid-back fishing village with black volcanic sand and a backdrop of Mount Agung. Amed is renowned for its excellent snorkeling and diving opportunities, with vibrant coral reefs and a variety of marine life to discover. Explore the underwater world, relax in the tranquil atmosphere, and immerse yourself in the local village life.

These are just a few of the stunning beaches Bali has to offer. From popular tourist spots to hidden gems, each beach has its own unique charm and beauty. Whether you're seeking adventure, relaxation, or simply a chance to soak up the sun, Bali's beaches will captivate you with their natural splendor and create memories that will last a lifetime.

Discovering Bali's Cultural Heritage

Bali, known as the "Island of the Gods," is not only blessed with natural beauty but also steeped in a rich cultural heritage. The island's unique blend of Hindu traditions, intricate architecture, vibrant festivals, and warm hospitality make it a fascinating destination for cultural exploration. In this chapter, we will delve into Bali's cultural heritage, highlighting some of the key aspects that make the island a truly captivating and culturally diverse place to visit.

Temples:

Bali is renowned for its thousands of temples, which are an integral part of the island's religious and cultural fabric. Each village has at least one temple, and larger towns are adorned with magnificent temples of historical significance. Pura Besakih, known as the "Mother Temple," is one of the most important and sacred temples in Bali. Situated on the slopes of Mount Agung, it offers breathtaking views and an insight into Bali's spiritual beliefs.

Traditional Balinese Architecture:

Balinese architecture is characterized by its intricate design, rich symbolism, and meticulous craftsmanship. The island is dotted with traditional compounds, known as "kampungs," showcasing stunning examples of Balinese architecture. The distinctive features include multi-tiered roofs, intricately carved wooden doors and pillars, and ornate stone carvings. Explore the royal palaces, such as Ubud Palace and Klungkung Palace, to witness the grandeur of Balinese architecture.

Balinese Dance and Music:

Bali's vibrant performing arts scene is a testament to its cultural richness. Traditional Balinese dances, such as the Barong, Legong, and Kecak, are not only visually captivating but also narrate ancient Hindu myths and epics. Attending a dance performance is a must for every visitor to Bali. The accompanying music, played on traditional instruments like the gamelan, creates a mesmerizing and immersive experience.

Ubud Art and Craft:

Ubud, the cultural heart of Bali, is a hub for art and craft enthusiasts. Explore the numerous galleries, art studios, and workshops showcasing traditional Balinese paintings, woodcarvings, silver jewelry, and intricate batik textiles. Visit the Blanco Renaissance Museum to admire the works of renowned Spanish artist Antonio Blanco, who made Bali his home.

Balinese Cuisine:

Indulge in the flavors of Balinese cuisine, which combines aromatic spices, fresh ingredients, and traditional cooking techniques. Try signature dishes such as Nasi Goreng (fried rice), Babi Guling (suckling pig), and Sate Lilit (minced meat satay). Traditional food markets, such as Pasar Badung in Denpasar, offer a glimpse into the local culinary scene, while cooking classes provide an opportunity to learn the secrets of Balinese cooking.

Galungan and Nyepi:

Experience the cultural festivities of Galungan and Nyepi, two of Bali's most important religious celebrations. Galungan marks the victory of good over evil and is characterized by beautifully decorated bamboo poles, traditional offerings, and vibrant processions. Nyepi, or the Day of Silence, is a unique cultural event where the entire island observes a day of silence, reflection, and fasting. It's a time to experience the tranquility and spiritual introspection that is deeply ingrained in Balinese culture.

Traditional Villages:

Venture beyond the tourist areas and explore Bali's traditional villages to witness the authentic rural life and cultural traditions. Tenganan Village, known for its ancient customs and traditional weaving, offers a glimpse into Bali's pre-Hindu past. Penglipuran Village showcases traditional architecture and community-based village life, while Trunyan Village offers a unique funeral ritual where bodies are placed under a sacred tree instead of being cremated or buried.

Melasti Rituals and Processions:

Witness the vibrant Melasti rituals and processions that take place along Bali's beaches in the lead-up to Nyepi. During this purification ceremony, Balinese Hindus gather by the sea to cleanse themselves spiritually and seek blessings from the gods. The atmosphere is filled with the sound of gamelan music, the fragrance of incense, and the colorful attire of the participants, creating a captivating and visually stunning experience.

Immerse yourself in Bali's cultural heritage, and you will discover a fascinating tapestry of rituals, art forms, traditions, and warm-hearted locals. The island's unique cultural offerings provide not just a vacation but a truly enriching and transformative experience.

Unforgettable Adventures in Bali

Bali, with its diverse landscapes and natural wonders, offers an array of exhilarating adventures for thrill-seekers and outdoor enthusiasts. From hiking to water sports, exploring underwater worlds to soaring above the treetops, the island presents endless opportunities for unforgettable experiences. In this chapter, we will explore some of the most thrilling adventures in Bali, ensuring that you make the most of your time on this adventure-filled island.

Mount Batur Sunrise Trek:

Embark on an early morning adventure to witness the breathtaking sunrise from the summit of Mount Batur. This active volcano offers a moderate hiking trail that takes you through lush landscapes and volcanic terrain. Reach the peak just in time to marvel at the stunning sunrise views, illuminating the surrounding mountains, caldera, and Lake Batur. It's a truly awe-inspiring experience that will stay with you forever.

White Water Rafting on Ayung River:

Challenge yourself with a white water rafting expedition along the Ayung River. Navigate through thrilling rapids and take in the lush jungle scenery surrounding the riverbanks. Rafting in Bali offers a perfect combination of adrenaline-pumping excitement and breathtaking natural beauty.

Scuba Diving and Snorkeling:

Explore the vibrant underwater world

surrounding Bali through scuba diving or snorkeling. The island boasts numerous dive sites teeming with colorful coral reefs, exotic marine life, and even shipwrecks to explore. Visit popular diving spots like Tulamben, Menjangan Island, or Nusa Penida, and witness the captivating beauty of Bali's underwater realm.

Bali Swing and Jungle Adventures:

Satisfy your craving for adrenaline at Bali Swing and Jungle Adventures, located in the lush jungles near Ubud. Swing above the treetops, soar through the air on zip lines, and conquer thrilling rope courses. Enjoy panoramic views of the surrounding landscapes and immerse yourself in the natural beauty while experiencing the rush of adventure.

ATV Quad Biking:

Embark on an off-road adventure with ATV quad biking through Bali's stunning landscapes. Ride through rice terraces, lush forests, and rural villages, experiencing the island's natural beauty up close. It's an exhilarating way to explore the less-traveled paths of Bali and discover hidden gems along the way.

Surfing:

Bali's world-class surf breaks attract surfers from around the globe. Whether you're a beginner or an experienced surfer, Bali offers waves for every skill level. Head to popular surf spots like Uluwatu, Padang Padang, or Canggu to catch the perfect wave or take surf lessons from local instructors to ride the waves like a pro.

Canyoning in Gitgit Waterfall:

Challenge yourself with canyoning, an adventure that combines trekking, rappelling, and swimming through the stunning Gitgit Waterfall. Navigate through narrow canyons, jump into natural pools, and rappel down waterfalls surrounded by lush tropical foliage. It's a thrilling experience that allows you to immerse yourself in Bali's stunning natural beauty.

Paragliding in Uluwatu:

Soar through the sky and witness Bali's stunning coastline from a bird's-eye view with paragliding in Uluwatu. Take off from the cliff tops and glide above the crystal-clear waters, enjoying the sensation of freedom and the breathtaking vistas below. It's an adventure that combines adrenaline with tranquility, offering a unique perspective of Bali's coastal landscapes.

Treetop Adventure Park:

Experience a treetop adventure at Bali Treetop Adventure Park in Bedugul. Swing, zip line, and navigate through suspended bridges and obstacles set amidst the lush canopy of trees. This family-friendly adventure park offers different circuits suitable for all ages, allowing everyone to unleash their inner adventurer.

Volcano Cycling Tour:

Embark on a cycling tour down the slopes of Mount Batur, taking in the mesmerizing views of the volcanic landscapes, rice terraces, and traditional villages. Cycle through scenic countryside and interact with friendly locals, immersing yourself in the island's rural charm.

These are just a few of the unforgettable adventures that await you in Bali. Whether you're seeking adrenaline-pumping experiences or immersive encounters with nature, Bali has something for everyone. Embark on these thrilling escapades and create memories that will last a lifetime.

Exploring Bali's Temples and Sacred Sites

Bali, often referred to as the "Island of a Thousand Temples," is renowned for its rich spiritual heritage and the multitude of temples and sacred sites that dot its landscape. These ancient structures not only serve as places of worship but also hold cultural, historical, and architectural significance. In this chapter, we will delve into the enchanting world of Bali's temples and sacred sites, guiding you through some of the most iconic and spiritually captivating locations on the island.

Pura Besakih:

Pura Besakih, also known as the "Mother Temple," is the largest and most important Hindu temple complex in Bali. Located on the slopes of Mount Agung, this magnificent site consists of over 20 separate temples, each dedicated to different deities and serving specific rituals. Explore the grandeur of Pura Besakih, marvel at the intricate stone carvings, and witness the breathtaking views of the surrounding mountains and rice terraces.

Tanah Lot:

Situated on a rocky outcrop along the southwestern coast of Bali, Tanah Lot is one of the most iconic and picturesque temples on the island. The temple is perched on a rock formation that becomes an island during high tide, creating a stunning sight against the backdrop of crashing waves. Experience the magical sunset views, witness traditional ceremonies, and soak in the spiritual ambiance of this unique temple.

Uluwatu Temple:

Perched on a cliff-top overlooking the Indian Ocean, Uluwatu Temple is not only a sacred site but also a popular destination for its dramatic location and enchanting Kecak dance performances. Explore the temple grounds, watch the mesmerizing sunset, and be enthralled by the rhythmic chanting and fire dance performance that takes place at the adjacent amphitheater.

Goa Gajah (Elephant Cave):

Discover the ancient archaeological site of Goa Gajah, also known as the Elephant Cave. Located near Ubud, this unique temple complex features a mysterious cave entrance adorned with intricate carvings of mythological creatures. Explore the hidden chambers, marvel at the bathing pools, and soak in the serene and spiritual atmosphere of this historical site.

Tirta Empul:

Tirta Empul is a sacred water temple located in the village of Tampaksiring. The temple is known for its holy spring, where Balinese Hindus come to cleanse themselves spiritually. Witness the purification rituals, join the locals in bathing in the holy waters, and experience the sense of serenity and renewal that Tirta Empul offers.

Ulun Danu Bratan:

Located on the shores of Lake Bratan in Bedugul, Ulun Danu Bratan is a picturesque temple dedicated to the goddess of the lake, Dewi

Danu. The temple's unique location, with the lake and surrounding mountains as a backdrop, creates a postcard-perfect scene. Explore the temple complex, stroll through the beautifully landscaped gardens, and enjoy the tranquility of this serene setting.

Pura Luhur Lempuyang:

Pura Luhur Lempuyang, nestled on the slopes of Mount Lempuyang, is known for its stunning gate, locally known as the "Gateway to Heaven." The gate frames the majestic view of Mount Agung and is a popular spot for capturing Instagram-worthy photos. Climb the staircase leading to the temple, immerse yourself in the spiritual atmosphere, and admire the panoramic vistas that unfold before you.

Pura Taman Ayun:

Pura Taman Ayun, located in Mengwi, is a beautiful temple complex surrounded by a moat and lush gardens. The temple's name translates to "Garden Temple in the Water," reflecting its tranquil setting. Explore the intricately carved gates, walk through the serene courtyard, and appreciate the harmonious Balinese architectural design that represents the harmony between humans and the divine.

Gunung Kawi:

Gunung Kawi is an ancient rock-cut temple complex carved into the cliffs near Tampaksiring. The site features monumental shrines dedicated to Balinese kings and queens from the 11th century.

Take a stroll through the lush valley, marvel at the towering stone monuments, and feel the spiritual energy that permeates this mystical place.

Pura Luhur Batukaru:

Nestled amidst the mist-shrouded slopes of Mount Batukaru, Pura Luhur Batukaru is one of Bali's most sacred temples. Surrounded by dense jungle and pristine nature, this temple offers a serene and peaceful retreat away from the bustling tourist areas. Immerse yourself in the spiritual ambience, take a meditative walk through the temple grounds, and connect with the tranquility of the natural surroundings.

Visiting Bali's temples and sacred sites is not just an exploration of religious and cultural heritage but also an opportunity to connect with the island's spiritual essence. Whether you seek architectural marvels, cultural insights, or a sense of tranquility, Bali's temples offer a truly enchanting journey into the heart and soul of the island.

Bali's Unique Traditional Arts and Crafts

Bali is renowned for its vibrant arts and crafts scene, where traditional skills are passed down through generations, resulting in exquisite works of art that capture the essence of Balinese culture. From intricate wood carvings to vibrant paintings, intricate silver jewelry to delicate textiles, the island is a treasure trove of creativity and craftsmanship. In this chapter, we will explore Bali's unique traditional arts and crafts, highlighting the techniques, symbolism, and cultural significance behind these remarkable creations.

Wood Carving:

Wood carving holds a prominent place in Bali's artistic heritage. Intricate sculptures and decorative panels can be found in temples, palaces, and traditional homes across the island. Balinese wood carvers possess exceptional skills in shaping wood into intricate patterns and lifelike figures, often depicting mythological creatures, deities, and scenes from Hindu epics. Visit the craft villages of Mas and Ubud to witness the masterful artistry of Balinese wood carving.

Batik:

Batik, a traditional Indonesian textile art form, is characterized by the intricate patterns created through a wax-resist dyeing technique. In Bali, batik is predominantly practiced in the village of Tohpati. Visit the workshops to witness the meticulous process of applying wax and dyeing the fabric to create stunning designs. Admire the vibrant colors and motifs that often depict Balinese mythology and folklore.

Silver Jewelry:

Bali has long been known for its exquisite silver jewelry, crafted by skilled artisans in the village of Celuk. Balinese silversmiths create intricate pieces using traditional techniques, including granulation and filigree work. Explore the workshops and galleries to find unique jewelry pieces adorned with intricate patterns, traditional motifs, and semi-precious gemstones.

Painting:

Bali's painting tradition dates back to the early 20th century when European artists were drawn to the island's natural beauty and vibrant culture. Balinese painters have since developed their distinctive style, blending traditional techniques with modern influences. Visit the art galleries in Ubud, Batuan, and Peliatan to admire the works of renowned artists and discover a diverse range of styles, from classical Balinese paintings to contemporary expressions.

Stone Carving:

Bali's stone carvers are known for their ability to transform blocks of stone into intricate sculptures and reliefs. The sculptures often depict deities, mythological creatures, and epic narratives. Explore the craft villages of Batubulan and Batuan to witness the art of stone carving and appreciate the skill and dedication required to create these awe-inspiring pieces.

Gamelan Music:

Gamelan music is an integral part of Bali's cultural heritage. It consists of a traditional ensemble of percussion instruments, including metallophones, gongs, drums, and bamboo flutes. Experience the enchanting melodies and rhythmic beats of Gamelan music during temple ceremonies, traditional performances, or even at specialized music schools that offer gamelan lessons.

Wayang Kulit:

Wayang Kulit, or shadow puppetry, is a traditional form of storytelling that combines intricate leather puppets, music, and narration. The puppeteer, known as a dalang, skillfully manipulates the puppets behind a white screen, casting their shadows to create a captivating visual narrative. Witness a Wayang Kulit performance to immerse yourself in this ancient art form and experience the tales of Balinese mythology and folklore.

Songket Weaving:

Songket is a traditional Balinese textile characterized by its intricately woven patterns, metallic threads, and vibrant colors. The weaving process is intricate, with the patterns often reflecting cultural symbols and local motifs. Visit the weaving villages of Sidemen and Tenganan to observe the skilled weavers in action and appreciate the mastery involved in creating these stunning textiles.

Bali's traditional arts and crafts not only showcase the island's immense creativity but also provide a window into its cultural heritage. Exploring these art forms allows you to appreciate the skill, dedication, and symbolism behind each creation, giving you a deeper understanding of Bali's rich artistic traditions. Whether you admire the delicate details of a wood carving, the vibrant colors of a painting, or the intricate patterns of a piece of jewelry, Bali's arts and crafts will leave you in awe of the island's exceptional craftsmanship.

Sampling Balinese Cuisine: A Food Lover's Guide

Bali is not only a paradise for its stunning landscapes and vibrant culture but also a culinary haven that offers a tantalizing array of flavors and dishes. Balinese cuisine is a delightful blend of aromatic spices, fresh ingredients, and traditional cooking techniques, resulting in a diverse and mouthwatering culinary experience. In this chapter, we will take you on a gastronomic journey through Balinese cuisine, exploring the unique flavors, iconic dishes, and must-try delicacies that will satisfy every food lover's palate.

Nasi Goreng:

No exploration of Balinese cuisine would be complete without trying Nasi Goreng, Indonesia's beloved fried rice dish. In Bali, Nasi Goreng is often prepared with a local twist, featuring aromatic spices, shrimp paste, and a variety of ingredients such as shrimp, chicken, or vegetables. Served with a side of pickles and a fried egg on top, Nasi Goreng is a flavorful and satisfying staple that can be found in almost every corner of the island.

Babi Guling:

Babi Guling, or suckling pig, is a legendary Balinese dish that showcases the island's love for pork. The pig is marinated with a blend of spices, including turmeric, coriander, lemongrass, and garlic, before being roasted to perfection, resulting in crispy skin and tender meat. Babi Guling is typically served with rice, lawar (a spicy vegetable salad), and sambal (spicy chili sauce). This iconic dish is a must-try for meat lovers seeking an authentic Balinese culinary experience.

Sate:

Sate, or satay, is a popular Indonesian street food that has become a staple in Bali's culinary scene. Skewered and grilled meat, such as chicken, pork, or beef, is marinated in a flavorful blend of spices, then grilled to perfection. Served with a rich peanut sauce and accompanied by rice cakes or lontong, sate is a delicious and satisfying snack that can be enjoyed any time of the day.

Lawar:

Lawar is a traditional Balinese dish that combines minced meat (usually pork or chicken), coconut, vegetables, and spices. The ingredients are mixed with blood to enhance the flavor and create a unique texture. Lawar is often served during religious ceremonies and special occasions, offering a distinctive taste of Balinese culinary traditions.

Bebek Betutu:

Bebek Betutu is a traditional Balinese dish that features slow-cooked duck marinated in a rich blend of spices, including turmeric, ginger, galangal, and chili. The duck is wrapped in banana leaves and then cooked for several hours until tender and flavorful. Bebek Betutu is usually served with steamed rice, sambal, and a side of fresh vegetables, providing a truly indulgent and aromatic dining experience.

Pepes:

Pepes refers to a cooking technique in which a mixture of meat, fish, or vegetables is wrapped in banana leaves and steamed or grilled. The banana leaves impart a unique aroma and flavor to the food, while the steaming process ensures that the ingredients remain moist and tender. Pepes can be found in various forms, with popular options including Pepes Ikan (steamed fish) and Pepes Ayam (steamed chicken).

Balinese Satay Lilit:

Balinese Satay Lilit is a variation of the classic satay, where the meat is finely minced and mixed with grated coconut, aromatic spices, and fresh herbs. The mixture is then wrapped around lemongrass or bamboo skewers and grilled over charcoal. Balinese Satay Lilit is known for its complex flavors and delightful texture, making it a favorite among locals and visitors alike.

Gado-Gado:

Gado-Gado is a refreshing and nutritious salad that features a mix of blanched vegetables, such as bean sprouts, green beans, cabbage, and tofu, topped with a rich peanut sauce. The combination of crunchy vegetables and creamy peanut sauce creates a harmonious blend of flavors and textures. Gado-Gado is a popular vegetarian dish in Bali and is often enjoyed as a light meal or a side dish.

Pisang Goreng:

Pisang Goreng, or fried banana, is a beloved

Indonesian dessert that has become a staple street food snack in Bali. Ripe bananas are coated in a batter made from flour, rice flour, and sometimes coconut milk, before being deep-fried until golden and crispy. Served hot, Pisang Goreng is a delightful treat that showcases the natural sweetness of bananas and is often enjoyed with a cup of tea or coffee.

Bubur Sumsum:

Bubur Sumsum is a traditional Indonesian rice flour porridge that is popular as a sweet dessert. The porridge is made by cooking rice flour with coconut milk and pandan leaves, resulting in a smooth and creamy texture. It is typically served with a palm sugar syrup and topped with grated coconut or fried shallots, creating a comforting and indulgent dessert.

Sampling Balinese cuisine is an adventure for the taste buds, allowing you to explore a diverse range of flavors and textures that reflect the island's rich culinary heritage. From savory dishes like Nasi Goreng and Babi Guling to sweet treats like Pisang Goreng and Bubur Sumsum, Bali's food scene offers something for every palate. So, indulge in the local flavors, seek out hidden food stalls and warungs (small restaurants), and savor the culinary delights that make Bali a true paradise for food lovers.

Exploring Bali's Vibrant Nightlife

When the sun sets in Bali, a whole new world comes alive. The island's vibrant nightlife offers a diverse range of entertainment options, from beachfront bars and nightclubs to cultural performances and sunset cruises. Whether you're seeking a lively party scene or a more relaxed evening of live music and cultural experiences, Bali has something for everyone. In this chapter, we will take you on a journey through Bali's vibrant nightlife, highlighting the best venues, events, and experiences that will make your evenings in Bali unforgettable.

Seminyak:

Seminyak is known for its bustling nightlife scene, offering a wide array of trendy bars, clubs, and beach clubs. Start your evening with a sunset cocktail at one of the beachfront bars like Ku De Ta or Potato Head Beach Club, where you can enjoy stunning views while sipping on refreshing drinks. As the night progresses, head to the lively clubs such as Jenja or La Favela, where you can dance the night away to the beats of international DJs.

Kuta:

Kuta is a hub for partygoers, offering an energetic atmosphere and a variety of nightlife options. The area is dotted with bars, pubs, and clubs that cater to different tastes and budgets. Enjoy live music performances at venues like Apache Reggae Bar or Hard Rock Cafe, where you can sing along to classic rock tunes. For a more lively experience, check out Sky Garden, a multi-level nightclub known for its energetic crowds and themed party nights.

Ubud:

While Ubud is known for its tranquil and spiritual ambiance, it also offers a unique nightlife experience. Explore the vibrant live music scene at places like Laughing Buddha Bar or No Mas Bar, where you can enjoy live bands playing various genres, including reggae, jazz, and rock. Don't miss the opportunity to catch a traditional Balinese dance performance, such as the mesmerizing Kecak Fire Dance, at the Ubud Palace or Pura Dalem Ubud.

Canggu:

Canggu has emerged as a trendy destination with a vibrant nightlife scene. Enjoy the laid-back atmosphere and beach vibes at venues like Old Man's or The Lawn, where you can relax with a drink and listen to live music as you watch the sunset. If you're looking for a more immersive experience, join a beach bonfire gathering or a silent disco event, where you can dance to the rhythm of your own headphones.

Nusa Dua:

Nusa Dua offers a more refined and upscale nightlife experience. Many of the luxury resorts in the area feature stylish bars and lounges where you can enjoy live music, specialty cocktails, and stunning ocean views. For a memorable evening, consider booking a sunset dinner cruise, where you can indulge in a delicious meal while sailing along Bali's picturesque coastline.

Cultural Performances:

Bali is renowned for its traditional arts and cultural performances, which are not to be missed during your visit. Experience the captivating Kecak dance at the Uluwatu Temple, where performers tell ancient Hindu tales through rhythmic chanting and synchronized movements. Other cultural performances, such as the Legong dance or the Barong dance, can be enjoyed at various venues across the island.

Night Markets:

For a taste of local cuisine and a lively atmosphere, explore Bali's night markets. These bustling markets offer a wide range of street food, snacks, and traditional dishes at affordable prices. The Sanur Night Market and Gianyar Night Market are popular choices, where you can sample Balinese delicacies like Nasi Campur (mixed rice), Sate Lilit (Balinese-style satay), and Pisang Goreng (fried banana).

Rooftop Bars:

Bali's skyline is adorned with rooftop bars that offer panoramic views and stylish settings. Enjoy a sophisticated evening at venues like Rock Bar Bali in Jimbaran or MoonLite Kitchen and Bar in Seminyak, where you can savor creative cocktails and gourmet cuisine while admiring the breathtaking vistas of the island.

Exploring Bali's vibrant nightlife is a must for those seeking excitement and entertainment during their visit. Whether you prefer the lively party scene, cultural performances, beachfront gatherings, or relaxing rooftop experiences, Bali offers a diverse range of options to suit every taste. So, embrace the energy of the island, immerse yourself in the lively atmosphere, and create unforgettable memories as you discover Bali's vibrant nightlife.

Wellness and Spa Retreats in Bali

Bali is not only a destination for stunning beaches and cultural experiences but also a haven for wellness and rejuvenation. The island is renowned for its world-class spa retreats that offer a serene and healing environment, combined with traditional healing practices and luxurious treatments. In this chapter, we will delve into the world of wellness and spa retreats in Bali, highlighting the top destinations and experiences that will nurture your body, mind, and soul.

Ubud:

Ubud, often referred to as the spiritual heart of Bali, is a hub for wellness and spa retreats. Surrounded by lush greenery and rice terraces, Ubud offers a tranquil setting that is perfect for relaxation and rejuvenation. Here, you can find a wide range of wellness centers and retreats that offer holistic treatments, yoga classes, meditation sessions, and healing therapies inspired by Balinese traditions. Popular retreats in Ubud include the Yoga Barn, Fivelements Retreat Bali, and the COMO Shambhala Estate.

Seminyak and Canggu:

If you prefer to combine wellness with a touch of luxury, Seminyak and Canggu are excellent choices. These coastal areas boast upscale resorts and spas that provide top-notch facilities and a range of indulgent treatments. From Balinese massages and body scrubs to rejuvenating facials and traditional healing therapies, you can pamper yourself with a wide array of options. Some notable wellness retreats in Seminyak and Canggu include the Amo Spa, the Away Bali Legian Camakila, and the Como Uma Canggu.

Nusa Dua:

Nusa Dua is known for its luxury resorts and pristine beaches, making it an ideal destination for a wellness retreat. Many resorts in Nusa Dua have their own spa facilities that offer a blend of Balinese and international treatments, including traditional massages, hot stone therapies, and body wraps. The tranquil environment, coupled with professional therapists and state-of-the-art facilities, ensures a truly rejuvenating experience. Some recommended wellness retreats in Nusa Dua are the Mulia Spa, the Ritz-Carlton Spa, and the Mandara Spa.

Healing Hot Springs:

Bali is also home to natural hot springs that are believed to possess healing properties. One such destination is Toya Devasya Hot Springs in Kintamani, where you can soak in mineral-rich hot springs while enjoying breathtaking views of Lake Batur and Mount Batur. These hot springs are said to have therapeutic effects on various health conditions and can be a soothing experience for both the body and mind.

Yoga and Meditation Retreats:

Bali is a haven for yoga and meditation enthusiasts, offering a range of retreats and centers dedicated to these practices. Whether you're a beginner or an experienced practitioner, you can find classes and retreats tailored to your needs. The island's serene environment and spiritual ambiance provide an ideal backdrop for deepening your practice and reconnecting with yourself. Some renowned yoga and meditation retreats in Bali include the Yoga Barn, the Bali Silent Retreat, and the Soulshine Bali.

Traditional Balinese Healing:

Bali is deeply rooted in ancient healing traditions, and experiencing a traditional Balinese healing session can be a transformative and deeply relaxing experience. Traditional healers, known as Balians, offer various therapies such as energy healing, herbal remedies, and intuitive readings. These sessions aim to restore balance and harmony to the body and promote overall well-being. It is important to approach traditional healing practices with respect and seek recommendations from reliable sources.

Organic Cuisine and Detox Programs:

Many wellness retreats in Bali emphasize the importance of nutrition and offer organic cuisine and detox programs. These programs focus on cleansing the body through nutritious meals, juices, and herbal remedies. The retreats often have their own organic gardens, where they grow fresh produce for their meals. Participating in a detox program can help rejuvenate your body, improve digestion, and increase energy levels.

Bali's wellness and spa retreats offer a

sanctuary of relaxation and rejuvenation, allowing you to escape the stresses of everyday life and focus on your well-being. Whether you seek traditional Balinese healing, yoga and meditation practices, luxurious spa treatments, or holistic wellness programs, Bali has something to cater to your needs. So, take the time to nourish your body, calm your mind, and revitalize your spirit as you immerse yourself in the wellness offerings of this enchanting island.

Family-Friendly Activities in Bali

Bali is not only a destination for romantic getaways and adventurous explorations but also a wonderful place for family vacations. The island offers a plethora of family-friendly activities that cater to both children and adults, ensuring that everyone in the family has a memorable and enjoyable experience. In this chapter, we will explore the top family-friendly activities in Bali that will keep the whole family entertained and create lasting memories.

Waterparks:

Bali is home to several exciting waterparks that guarantee hours of fun for the whole family. Waterbom Bali in Kuta is one of the island's most popular waterparks, featuring thrilling slides, lazy rivers, and splash pools suitable for all ages. Another fantastic option is Circus Waterpark in Kuta, which offers a range of water attractions and a dedicated kids' zone with age-appropriate rides.

Bali Safari and Marine Park:

The Bali Safari and Marine Park is an incredible destination that allows families to get up close and personal with a wide range of animals from around the world. Take a safari journey through the park, where you can encounter majestic elephants, lions, zebras, and more. The park also features animal shows, a water park, and opportunities for interactive experiences like feeding the animals.

Bali Treetop Adventure Park:

Located in Bedugul, the Bali Treetop Adventure Park offers an exhilarating experience for the whole family. The park features a series of treetop circuits with varying levels of difficulty, allowing participants to navigate through suspended bridges, zip lines, and other challenging obstacles. It's a great opportunity for both children and adults to test their agility and enjoy an exciting adventure amidst the lush greenery.

Bali Bird Park:

For nature and bird lovers, the Bali Bird Park in Gianyar is a must-visit. The park is home to over a thousand species of birds, including rare and endangered ones. Families can take a leisurely stroll through beautifully landscaped gardens and interact with the feathered residents. The park also offers educational shows and feeding sessions, providing a unique and educational experience for children.

Bali Zoo:

The Bali Zoo offers a fantastic opportunity to observe and learn about various animals. Families can enjoy up-close encounters with animals like orangutans, tigers, and crocodiles. The zoo also organizes a range of activities, such as animal feeding, animal shows, and even night safaris, allowing visitors to experience the zoo's vibrant atmosphere after dark.

Surfing Lessons:

Bali is renowned for its world-class surfing spots, and taking surfing lessons can be a thrilling experience for the whole family. Several surf schools offer lessons specifically designed for beginners and children, providing a safe and enjoyable introduction to riding the waves. Places like Kuta Beach and Seminyak Beach are ideal for beginners, with gentle waves and experienced instructors to guide you.

Balinese Cooking Classes:

Immerse your family in Balinese culture and cuisine by participating in a cooking class together. Many cooking schools in Bali offer family-friendly classes where you can learn to prepare traditional Balinese dishes using fresh local ingredients. From making satay to crafting traditional desserts, the cooking classes provide an interactive and educational experience that will delight the taste buds of the entire family.

Bali Tree House Adventure Park:

Located in the picturesque region of Bedugul, the Bali Tree House Adventure Park is a thrilling experience for families seeking adventure. The park features a series of tree houses connected by hanging bridges and zip lines, allowing you to navigate through the treetops and enjoy breathtaking views of the surrounding forests. It's an adrenaline-pumping activity that combines the beauty of nature with an element of excitement.

Turtle Conservation and Release:

Engage in a meaningful and educational experience by visiting a turtle conservation center in Bali. These centers focus on the conservation and protection of sea turtles, and visitors can learn about the lifecycle of these incredible creatures. Some centers even offer the opportunity to participate in turtle releases, where you can witness the turtles being returned to the ocean. It's a truly special experience that will leave a lasting impact on the whole family.

Beach Picnics and Water Sports:

Bali's stunning beaches provide a perfect backdrop for family picnics and water sports activities. Pack a delicious picnic and head to one of the tranquil beaches, such as Nusa Dua or Sanur, where the whole family can relax, swim, and build sandcastles. Additionally, you can engage in water sports activities like banana boating, snorkeling, and jet skiing, creating exciting moments and treasured memories.

Bali offers a wealth of family-friendly activities that cater to different interests and age groups. Whether you're seeking thrilling adventures, educational experiences, or simply quality time together, Bali has something to offer. Embrace the island's natural beauty, cultural heritage, and warm hospitality as you embark on a memorable family vacation in Bali.

Surfing and Water Sports in Bali

Bali is a surfer's paradise and a haven for water sports enthusiasts. With its warm tropical waters, consistent waves, and stunning coastline, the island offers a wide range of opportunities for surfing and various water sports. Whether you're a beginner looking to catch your first wave or an experienced surfer seeking a thrilling challenge, Bali has something for everyone. In this chapter, we will explore the exciting world of surfing and water sports in Bali, highlighting the top spots and activities that will get your adrenaline pumping.

Surfing:

Bali is renowned worldwide for its incredible surf breaks, attracting surfers from all corners of the globe. From beginners to professionals, there are waves suitable for every skill level. Some of the most popular surfing spots in Bali include:

Kuta Beach: Located in the bustling town of Kuta, this beach offers gentle and consistent waves, making it an ideal spot for beginners and those looking to improve their skills.

Uluwatu: Known for its world-class reef break, Uluwatu is a paradise for experienced surfers. The waves here can reach impressive heights, providing an exhilarating challenge.

Canggu: This coastal village boasts several breaks suitable for different levels of surfers. Berawa Beach and Batu Bolong Beach are great spots for beginners, while Echo Beach offers more challenging waves for intermediate and advanced surfers.

Padang Padang: Famous for its stunning beauty and powerful left-hand barrel, Padang Padang is a must-visit for experienced surfers looking for a thrilling ride.

Stand-Up Paddleboarding (SUP):

Stand-up paddleboarding has gained popularity in Bali in recent years, offering a fun and versatile water activity for all ages. Whether you're cruising along calm coastal waters or exploring the tranquil lakes and rivers of the island's interior, SUP allows you to enjoy the beauty of Bali from a unique perspective. SUP lessons and rentals are available at various surf schools and water sports centers across the island.

Jet Skiing:

For those seeking a high-speed water adventure, jet skiing is a fantastic option. Rent a jet ski and ride the waves, feeling the rush of adrenaline as you navigate through the open ocean. Tanjung Benoa, located on Bali's southeastern coast, is a popular area for jet skiing, with its calm waters and designated jet ski zones.

Parasailing:

Get a bird's-eye view of Bali's coastline by trying parasailing. Strapped into a harness and attached to a colorful parachute, you will be lifted high above the water and pulled by a speedboat. Enjoy the breathtaking panoramic views as you glide through the sky, feeling the wind in your hair. Parasailing is available at various beaches, including Tanjung Benoa and Nusa Dua.

Scuba Diving and Snorkeling:

Bali's crystal-clear waters teem with vibrant marine life, making it a perfect destination for scuba diving and snorkeling. Explore colorful coral reefs, encounter tropical fish, and even discover underwater statues and shipwrecks. Some of the top diving and snorkeling spots in Bali include Tulamben, Amed, Menjangan Island, and Nusa Penida. Dive centers and snorkeling tours can arrange trips suitable for both beginners and experienced divers.

White Water Rafting:

For an exhilarating adventure off the beaten path, head to Bali's rivers for white water rafting. Navigate through the rapids, cascading waterfalls, and lush jungle scenery as you paddle downstream. The Ayung River and Telaga Waja River are popular rafting locations, offering different levels of difficulty to cater to various skill levels.

Flyboarding:

Experience the thrill of flying above the water with flyboarding, a relatively new water sport in Bali. Strap on a water-powered jetpack attached to your feet and soar into the air, propelled by water pressure. It's a unique and adrenaline-pumping activity that will give you a sense of weightlessness and make you feel like a superhero.

Wakeboarding and Waterskiing:

Bali's calm bays and lakes provide excellent conditions for wakeboarding and waterskiing.

Skim across the water's surface, performing tricks and jumps as you're pulled by a boat. Whether you're a seasoned pro or a first-timer, Bali's water sports centers offer rentals and lessons to cater to all skill levels.

When participating in water sports in Bali, it's important to prioritize safety and choose reputable operators that provide proper equipment and guidance. Additionally, be mindful of local regulations and environmental conservation efforts to help preserve Bali's natural beauty for future generations to enjoy.

Surfing and water sports in Bali offer an exhilarating way to enjoy the island's natural beauty and make unforgettable memories. Whether you're riding the waves, exploring underwater wonders, or engaging in high-speed adventures, Bali's aquatic playground will captivate and thrill water sports enthusiasts of all ages and skill levels.

Hiking and Nature Treks in Bali

Bali is not just about beautiful beaches and vibrant culture; it is also home to stunning natural landscapes and breathtaking mountains. The island offers a variety of hiking trails and nature treks that allow visitors to immerse themselves in its lush greenery, discover hidden waterfalls, and witness panoramic views from towering peaks. In this chapter, we will explore the diverse hiking and nature trek options in Bali, highlighting the top trails that will take you on an unforgettable journey through the island's natural wonders.

Mount Batur Sunrise Trek:

One of the most popular hiking experiences in Bali is the Mount Batur sunrise trek. Mount Batur is an active volcano located in the Kintamani region, and the trek to its summit offers breathtaking views and an incredible sunrise experience. The trek usually begins early in the morning, as you make your way up the volcanic slopes in the darkness with the help of a local guide. Once you reach the summit, you will be rewarded with a stunning sunrise over the surrounding mountains and the shimmering Lake Batur below.

Mount Agung Trek:

For more experienced hikers seeking a challenge, Mount Agung, Bali's highest volcano, offers a rewarding climb. The trek to the summit is physically demanding but offers an incredible sense of accomplishment and panoramic views from the highest point on the island. It is recommended to undertake this trek with a knowledgeable guide due to the steep terrain and changing weather conditions.

Campuhan Ridge Walk:

Located in the artistic town of Ubud, the Campuhan Ridge Walk is a scenic trek that takes you through picturesque rice fields and lush river valleys. The trail starts near the Campuhan Bridge and meanders along a ridge, offering breathtaking views of the surrounding landscape. It's an easy and enjoyable walk suitable for all fitness levels, allowing you to appreciate the natural beauty of Bali's countryside.

Sekumpul Waterfall Trek:

Embark on an adventure to discover one of Bali's most stunning waterfalls, the Sekumpul Waterfall. Located in the northern region of Bali, this trek takes you through lush jungles and terraced rice fields to reach a cluster of majestic waterfalls cascading down a steep ravine. The trek can be challenging at times, but the reward of witnessing the power and beauty of Sekumpul Waterfall is worth every step.

Gitgit Waterfall Trek:

Another popular waterfall trek is the Gitgit Waterfall trek, which allows you to explore a series of enchanting waterfalls in Bali's central highlands. The trail leads you through tropical rainforests and small villages, providing a glimpse into the island's rural life. The highlight of the trek is the majestic

Gitgit Waterfall, surrounded by lush vegetation and a cool pool inviting you for a refreshing swim.

Jatiluwih Rice Terrace Trek:

Jatiluwih is a UNESCO World Heritage Site and is famous for its stunning terraced rice fields. Embark on a trek through this picturesque landscape, as you follow narrow paths that wind through the vibrant green fields. The trek offers a glimpse into traditional rice farming practices and allows you to appreciate the harmonious relationship between nature and agriculture in Bali.

Munduk Village Trek:

Munduk, located in the central highlands of Bali, is a serene mountain village known for its scenic beauty and cool climate. A trek through the surrounding hills and plantations takes you to hidden waterfalls, coffee and clove plantations, and stunning viewpoints. Immerse yourself in the tranquility of the countryside as you explore the lush vegetation and enjoy the fresh mountain air.

West Bali National Park Trek:

For nature lovers, a trek through the West Bali National Park is a must-do experience. This protected area is home to diverse ecosystems, including rainforests, mangrove forests, and coral reefs. Join a guided trek and discover the park's rich biodiversity, spot wildlife such as monkeys and deer, and explore pristine beaches and hidden coves.

When embarking on a hiking or nature trek in Bali, it's important to come prepared with suitable footwear, sun protection, plenty of water, and respect for the environment. Additionally, engaging the services of a knowledgeable guide ensures your safety and allows you to gain insights into the local flora, fauna, and cultural significance of the area.

Hiking and nature treks in Bali offer a unique opportunity to connect with the island's natural beauty and explore its diverse landscapes. Whether you're seeking adventure, tranquility, or a sense of accomplishment, Bali's hiking trails will take you on a journey of discovery and create lasting memories of your time on this enchanting island.

Diving and Snorkeling in Bali's Underwater Paradise

Bali is renowned for its vibrant and diverse marine life, making it a haven for diving and snorkeling enthusiasts. With its crystal-clear waters, colorful coral reefs, and abundant marine species, the island offers an unforgettable underwater experience. Whether you're a certified diver or a beginner snorkeler, Bali's underwater paradise has something to offer everyone. In this chapter, we will explore the top diving and snorkeling spots in Bali, highlighting the unique marine ecosystems and the incredible encounters that await beneath the surface.

Tulamben:

Located on Bali's northeast coast, Tulamben is famous for its stunning wreck dive site, the USAT Liberty Shipwreck. This World War II cargo ship lies close to the shore and is now home to a rich variety of coral and marine life. Divers can explore the wreckage and encounter schools of colorful fish, sea turtles, and even occasional sightings of larger marine creatures like reef sharks.

Amed:

Amed, also situated on Bali's northeast coast, offers a relaxed and laid-back diving and snorkeling experience. The area features beautiful coral gardens, vibrant marine life, and the chance to encounter exotic species such as pygmy seahorses and ghost pipefish. Amed's calm waters and shallow reefs make it an ideal spot for beginners to explore the underwater world.

Menjangan Island:

Part of West Bali National Park, Menjangan Island is a diving and snorkeling paradise. Its pristine coral reefs boast a rich biodiversity, including colorful coral formations, tropical fish, and unique marine creatures. The island's calm waters and excellent visibility make it a perfect destination for both experienced divers and snorkelers. Don't miss the famous underwater temple, known as Pura Underwater, which adds a touch of cultural intrigue to your underwater adventure.

Nusa Penida:

Located southeast of Bali, Nusa Penida offers some of the most thrilling and memorable diving experiences in the region. This rugged island is known for its encounters with majestic manta rays, which can be observed up close at sites like Manta Point. Nusa Penida is also home to the famous Crystal Bay, where divers can spot the elusive Mola Mola (sunfish) during the appropriate season. With its strong currents and challenging conditions, diving in Nusa Penida is recommended for more experienced divers.

Nusa Lembongan and Nusa Ceningan:

These neighboring islands offer a tranquil and picturesque setting for diving and snorkeling. The waters surrounding Nusa Lembongan and Nusa Ceningan are teeming with marine life, including vibrant coral gardens, tropical fish, and occasional encounters with sea turtles. The popular dive sites of Blue Corner and Mangrove Point offer thrilling drift dives with the possibility of seeing reef sharks and rays.

Padang Bai:

Located on Bali's east coast, Padang Bai is a charming village that serves as a gateway to several fantastic dive sites. The Blue Lagoon and Bias Tugal (also known as White Sand Beach) are popular spots for snorkeling, where you can swim among colorful fish and explore shallow coral reefs. Divers can also venture to nearby dive sites, including the famous dive site of the Shark Point, where sightings of blacktip reef sharks are common.

Seraya Secrets:

For macro photography enthusiasts, Seraya Secrets, located on Bali's northeast coast, is a hidden gem. This dive site offers excellent opportunities to spot rare critters such as frogfish, nudibranchs, and colorful shrimp. The site's diverse and abundant marine life, coupled with its unique black sand bottom, make it a must-visit spot for underwater photographers and critter lovers.

When planning a diving or snorkeling adventure in Bali, it's essential to choose a reputable dive center or tour operator that prioritizes safety and follows responsible diving practices. Ensure your equipment is in good condition, listen to the briefing provided by your guide, and be mindful of the marine environment by practicing good buoyancy control and avoiding contact with coral.

Diving and snorkeling in Bali's underwater paradise is a truly magical experience. Whether you're exploring vibrant coral reefs, encountering majestic marine creatures, or capturing the beauty of the underwater world through a camera lens, Bali's waters offer a world of wonder and excitement for water enthusiasts of all skill levels. Dive in and discover the incredible biodiversity that awaits beneath the surface.

Exploring Bali's Rice Terraces and Countryside

Bali's stunning rice terraces and picturesque countryside offer a glimpse into the island's traditional agricultural practices and breathtaking natural beauty. From cascading emerald-green fields to charming villages nestled in lush valleys, the rural landscapes of Bali are a feast for the eyes and a testament to the island's rich cultural heritage. In this chapter, we will delve into the top rice terraces and countryside destinations in Bali, inviting you to embark on a journey of exploration and appreciation for the island's agrarian roots.

Tegalalang Rice Terrace:

Located just north of Ubud, the Tegalalang Rice Terrace is one of Bali's most iconic and photographed landscapes. The terraced rice fields stretch across rolling hills, creating a mesmerizing panorama that showcases the harmony between nature and agriculture. Take a leisurely walk through the terraces, soak in the peaceful atmosphere, and learn about the traditional subak irrigation system that has sustained Bali's rice farming for centuries.

Jatiluwih Rice Terrace:

Recognized as a UNESCO World Heritage Site, the Jatiluwih Rice Terrace in Tabanan regency is a testament to Bali's ancient agricultural traditions. This vast expanse of terraced rice fields set against the backdrop of Mount Batukaru offers a breathtaking sight. Immerse yourself in the tranquility of the area as you wander through the terraces, interact with local farmers, and gain insights into the intricate processes of rice cultivation.

Sidemen Valley:

Nestled in the eastern part of Bali, the Sidemen Valley is a hidden gem that showcases the island's rural charm. The valley is dotted with verdant rice terraces, traditional villages, and the majestic presence of Mount Agung in the distance. Embark on a cycling or walking tour through the countryside, explore the local craft villages, and savor the untouched beauty of this idyllic landscape.

Pejeng Village:

Located near Ubud, Pejeng Village offers a glimpse into Bali's traditional village life and serene countryside. This charming village is known for its lush rice fields, ancient temples, and historic sites such as the Moon of Pejeng, the largest bronze kettle drum in Southeast Asia. Stroll through the village's narrow paths, interact with friendly locals, and witness daily rituals and ceremonies that are an integral part of Balinese culture.

Munduk:

Situated in the central highlands of Bali, Munduk is a cool and tranquil mountain village renowned for its breathtaking landscapes and scenic rice terraces. Embark on a trek through the surrounding hills, explore hidden waterfalls, and marvel at the panoramic views of the lush countryside. Munduk's pleasant climate and abundant natural beauty make it an ideal destination for nature lovers and those seeking a peaceful retreat.

Pupuan:

Pupuan, located in West Bali, is a lesser-known destination that offers a serene escape from the bustling tourist areas. The area is characterized by terraced rice fields, rolling hills, and a laid-back atmosphere. Visit the Belimbing rice terraces, where you can witness the traditional farming methods still practiced by local farmers. Pupuan's untouched beauty and tranquil ambiance provide a perfect opportunity to unwind and reconnect with nature.

Bangli:

Bangli, a regency in central Bali, is home to some of the island's most beautiful countryside landscapes. The regency is renowned for its terraced rice fields, picturesque lakes, and lush greenery. Explore the stunning landscapes of the Kintamani region, visit the serene Lake Batur, and hike to the summit of Mount Batur for breathtaking views of the surrounding countryside.

When exploring Bali's rice terraces and countryside, it's important to respect the local communities and their way of life. Dress modestly, seek permission before entering private property, and follow any guidelines provided by local farmers or guides. Engage with the locals, learn about their farming techniques, and perhaps even participate in the rice harvesting process during the planting or harvesting season.

Bali's rice terraces and countryside provide a serene and enchanting escape from the bustling coastal areas. Whether you're seeking tranquility, cultural immersion, or simply a connection with nature, the island's rural landscapes offer a captivating journey into Bali's agricultural heritage and the timeless beauty of its countryside.

Shopping in Bali: Markets, Boutiques, and More

Bali is a shopper's paradise, offering a diverse array of shopping experiences that range from vibrant markets to upscale boutiques. From unique handicrafts and traditional textiles to trendy fashion, jewelry, and homeware, the island's shopping scene caters to every taste and budget. In this chapter, we will explore the top shopping destinations in Bali, guiding you through the bustling markets, charming boutiques, and hidden gems where you can find the perfect souvenirs and treasures to bring back home.

Ubud Art Market:

Located in the heart of Ubud, the Ubud Art Market is a must-visit destination for art enthusiasts and bargain hunters. The market is filled with stalls offering a wide variety of traditional handicrafts, including hand-carved wooden masks, intricate silver jewelry, batik clothing, and Balinese paintings. Put your bargaining skills to the test and immerse yourself in the vibrant atmosphere of this iconic market.

Seminyak:

For a more upscale shopping experience, head to Seminyak, known for its trendy boutiques, high-end fashion, and designer homeware. The streets of Jalan Kayu Aya and Jalan Petitenget are lined with stylish shops featuring local and international brands, showcasing the latest fashion trends and unique pieces. Explore the upscale shopping complexes such as Seminyak Village and Seminyak Square, where you'll find a curated selection of boutique stores.

Sukawati Art Market:

Located in the village of Sukawati, just a short drive from Ubud, the Sukawati Art Market is a treasure trove of traditional Balinese arts and crafts. The market is renowned for its exquisite wood carvings, intricate stone sculptures, handwoven textiles, and traditional Balinese ceremonial items. Take your time to browse through the stalls, admire the craftsmanship, and discover unique pieces that capture the essence of Balinese culture.

Kuta Beachwalk:

Situated in the popular tourist area of Kuta, the Kuta Beachwalk offers a modern and vibrant shopping experience. This open-air mall features a mix of international brands, local boutiques, restaurants, and entertainment options. Enjoy a leisurely stroll along the promenade, indulge in some retail therapy, and relax in one of the many cafes or restaurants overlooking the beach.

Canggu:

Canggu has emerged as a hip and trendy destination in Bali, attracting a vibrant community of designers, artists, and entrepreneurs. Explore the streets of Jalan Batu Bolong and Jalan Pantai Berawa, where you'll find an eclectic mix of boutique shops, concept stores, and local artisan studios. Discover unique fashion, handmade jewelry, bohemian homeware, and stylish surfwear in this vibrant and artistic enclave.

Tegallalang Handicraft Center:

Situated near the famous Tegalalang Rice Terrace, the Tegallalang Handicraft Center offers an immersive shopping experience. Here, you can witness skilled artisans at work, creating intricate wood carvings, stone sculptures, and traditional Balinese crafts. Take the opportunity to interact with the artists, learn about their techniques, and acquire one-of-a-kind pieces directly from the source.

Pasar Badung:

Located in Denpasar, the capital city of Bali, Pasar Badung is the largest traditional market on the island. This bustling market is a sensory delight, with stalls overflowing with fresh produce, spices, textiles, and household items. Explore the market's vibrant alleys, sample local snacks, and experience the authentic atmosphere of daily Balinese life.

When shopping in Bali, it's important to hone your bargaining skills and be mindful of your budget. While bargaining is common in markets, be respectful and remember that a fair price benefits both the buyer and the seller. Additionally, consider the customs regulations of your home country when purchasing unique items such as antiques or artwork to ensure a smooth return journey.

Bali's shopping scene offers a blend of

tradition and modernity, providing an opportunity to immerse yourself in the island's rich artistic heritage while also indulging in contemporary fashion and design. Whether you're seeking cultural artifacts, fashionable clothing, or unique souvenirs, Bali's markets, boutiques, and shopping centers are sure to fulfill your retail desires.

Experiencing Balinese Festivals and Celebrations

Bali is a land of vibrant culture and rich traditions, and one of the best ways to immerse yourself in the island's cultural tapestry is by participating in its colorful festivals and celebrations. From grand processions and mesmerizing dances to elaborate ceremonies and spiritual rituals, Balinese festivals offer a unique insight into the island's spiritual beliefs, artistic expressions, and communal bonds. In this chapter, we will explore some of the most significant festivals and celebrations in Bali, inviting you to witness the beauty, energy, and spiritual essence of these extraordinary events.

Nyepi (Day of Silence):

Nyepi, also known as the Balinese New Year, is a unique and significant festival that marks a day of silence and self-reflection. The entire island comes to a complete standstill as the Balinese people observe a day of silence, fasting, and meditation. It is a time for introspection and purification, with no activities, lights, or entertainment allowed. Witness the surreal experience of an entire island in complete silence, as the Balinese respect this sacred day.

Galungan and Kuningan:

Galungan is a major Hindu festival that celebrates the victory of good over evil. It occurs every 210 days and lasts for ten days. The festival is marked by ornately decorated bamboo poles called "penjor" adorning the streets and temples, symbolizing gratitude for the bounties of the earth. The festivities include vibrant processions, traditional dances, and visits to family temples. The celebration concludes with Kuningan, a day of prayers and offerings to ancestors.

Saraswati Day:

Saraswati Day is dedicated to the Hindu goddess of knowledge, arts, and learning. On this day, the Balinese pay homage to Saraswati by participating in special ceremonies and offering prayers at temples and educational institutions. The Balinese people dress in their finest traditional attire, and students bring their books to receive blessings for knowledge and wisdom. Witness the devotion and reverence displayed during this auspicious day.

Odalan:

Odalan is a temple anniversary celebration that takes place throughout the year in various temples across Bali. Each temple has its own unique anniversary date based on the Balinese calendar. During Odalan, the temple comes alive with vibrant decorations, traditional music, dance performances, and religious ceremonies. Join the festivities and witness the deep spiritual devotion of the Balinese as they honor their ancestral temples.

Ubud Writers and Readers Festival:

For literature enthusiasts, the Ubud Writers and Readers Festival is a highlight on Bali's cultural calendar. Held annually in Ubud, this festival brings together renowned writers, thinkers, and artists from around the world for a week of discussions, workshops, and performances. Immerse yourself in the world of literature, engage in intellectual conversations, and gain insights into the diverse literary traditions of Bali and beyond.

Bali Arts Festival:

The Bali Arts Festival is a month-long celebration of the island's rich artistic heritage. Held annually from June to July, this festival showcases a multitude of cultural performances, including traditional dances, music, puppetry, and theatrical shows. Explore the vibrant exhibitions, witness the colorful parades, and marvel at the extraordinary talents of Balinese artists. It's an opportunity to experience the depth and diversity of Balinese arts and culture.

Melasti:

Melasti is a purification ritual that takes place a few days before Nyepi. It involves a procession to the beach or sacred water sources, where the Balinese people cleanse themselves and the sacred objects used in ceremonies. Witness the spectacle of thousands of Balinese dressed in traditional attire, carrying sacred items, and chanting prayers as they make their way to the water. It's a deeply spiritual and visually captivating experience.

Tumpek:

Tumpek is a series of special days dedicated to various aspects of Balinese life, such as animals, musical instruments, and plants. Tumpek Kandang, for example, is a day to honor domestic animals, while Tumpek Krulut celebrates traditional musical instruments. These days are marked by special ceremonies and offerings, showcasing the Balinese people's reverence for the natural world and their close connection to it.

When participating in Balinese festivals and celebrations, it's essential to respect the local customs and traditions. Dress modestly, be mindful of your behavior, and seek guidance from the locals to fully understand the significance of the rituals and ceremonies. By immersing yourself in these cultural festivities, you will gain a deeper appreciation for the spiritual heritage and vibrant community of Bali.

Day Trips and Excursions from Bali

While Bali offers a wealth of attractions and activities, the island's central location in the Indonesian archipelago also makes it an excellent base for exploring the surrounding areas. From pristine islands and majestic volcanoes to ancient temples and traditional villages, there are numerous day trips and excursions from Bali that allow you to venture beyond the island's borders and discover the beauty and diversity of the region. In this chapter, we will highlight some of the most popular day trips and excursions from Bali, giving you the opportunity to embark on unforgettable adventures and create lasting memories.

Nusa Penida:

Located just off the southeast coast of Bali, Nusa Penida is a paradise for nature enthusiasts and adventure seekers. Known for its stunning cliffs, crystal-clear waters, and pristine beaches, the island offers opportunities for snorkeling, diving, and hiking. Explore iconic landmarks such as Kelingking Beach, Angel's Billabong, and Crystal Bay. Take a day trip or spend a few days exploring this captivating island.

Mount Batur:

For breathtaking panoramic views and an exhilarating trekking experience, consider a day trip to Mount Batur. Located in the highlands of Bali, this active volcano offers a challenging yet rewarding hike to its summit. Start your journey before dawn to witness the mesmerizing sunrise over the surrounding landscapes and enjoy a well-deserved breakfast cooked using volcanic steam. The trek is guided, ensuring your safety and providing insightful information about the volcano and its significance in Balinese culture.

Ubud and its Surroundings:

While Ubud is a popular destination in its own right, the surrounding areas offer additional opportunities for exploration. Visit the Tegalalang Rice Terrace, known for its stunning terraced landscapes. Explore the sacred Monkey Forest Sanctuary, where you can observe playful monkeys and visit ancient temples. Discover traditional villages such as Celuk, known for its silver jewelry, and Mas, famous for its woodcarving. Immerse yourself in the artistic and cultural heart of Bali.

Gilli Islands:

Escape to the idyllic Gilli Islands, a group of three small islands located off the northwest coast of Lombok. These islands, namely Gili Trawangan, Gili Air, and Gili Meno, are known for their white sandy beaches, turquoise waters, and vibrant marine life. Go snorkeling or diving to explore colorful coral reefs and encounter turtles, tropical fish, and other marine species. Enjoy the laid-back island atmosphere and unwind in the picturesque surroundings.

Tanah Lot and Uluwatu:

Visit two of Bali's most iconic sea temples, Tanah Lot and Uluwatu, on a day trip along the southwestern coast of the island. Tanah Lot is perched on a rocky outcrop and is particularly famous for its stunning sunset views. Uluwatu Temple, situated atop a cliff, offers breathtaking panoramic vistas of the Indian Ocean. Both temples are revered as important spiritual sites and showcase the architectural splendor of Balinese temple design.

Tirta Gangga and Taman Ujung:

Experience the tranquility of Bali's water palaces by visiting Tirta Gangga and Taman Ujung. Tirta Gangga, located in East Bali, is a beautiful water palace renowned for its ornamental ponds, fountains, and lush gardens. Taman Ujung, also known as the Taman Soekasada Ujung, is another stunning water palace featuring a blend of Balinese and European architectural styles. Explore these serene locations, stroll through their serene gardens, and admire the intricate water features.

Jatiluwih Rice Terrace and Bedugul:

Embark on a journey to Bali's cultural and natural landscapes by visiting the Jatiluwih Rice Terrace and the scenic highland area of Bedugul. The Jatiluwih Rice Terrace, a UNESCO World Heritage site, offers expansive views of terraced rice fields nestled in the lush mountains. In Bedugul, explore the picturesque Ulun Danu Beratan Temple, located on the shores of Lake Beratan, and visit the Bali Botanic Garden, home to a diverse collection of tropical plants.

East Bali Exploration:

Venture off the beaten path and discover the tranquil beauty of East Bali. Explore the ancient village of Tenganan, known for its unique indigenous culture and traditional weaving techniques. Visit the Tirta Gangga Water Palace and the Besakih Temple, Bali's largest and most important Hindu temple complex. Immerse yourself in the scenic landscapes, traditional village life, and spiritual ambiance of this lesser-explored region.

When planning day trips and excursions from Bali, consider your interests, time constraints, and preferred modes of transportation. Whether you seek adventure, cultural exploration, or natural beauty, the surrounding areas of Bali offer a plethora of options to cater to every traveler's preferences. Embark on these excursions and uncover the diverse wonders that await just beyond the shores of Bali.

Sustainable Tourism in Bali

Bali, known for its natural beauty, rich cultural heritage, and warm hospitality, has become a popular tourist destination. With this increased tourism, there is a growing awareness of the importance of sustainable practices to protect the island's fragile ecosystems, preserve its cultural traditions, and ensure the well-being of local communities. Sustainable tourism in Bali is about promoting responsible travel that minimizes negative impacts while maximizing the positive contributions to the environment, society, and economy. In this chapter, we will explore various aspects of sustainable tourism in Bali and how travelers can contribute to preserving the island's unique charm for future generations.

Environmental Conservation:

Bali is blessed with stunning landscapes, including lush forests, pristine beaches, and terraced rice fields. To preserve these natural treasures, sustainable tourism practices encourage responsible behaviors such as minimizing waste and pollution, conserving water and energy, and supporting initiatives that protect biodiversity. Travelers can participate in beach cleanups, choose eco-friendly accommodations, and opt for nature-based activities that promote environmental conservation.

Cultural Preservation:

The cultural heritage of Bali is deeply intertwined with its natural surroundings.

Sustainable tourism emphasizes the preservation of the island's cultural traditions, arts, and rituals. Travelers are encouraged to engage respectfully with local communities, learn about their customs and traditions, and support cultural initiatives such as attending traditional performances and purchasing authentic local handicrafts. By respecting and valuing Bali's cultural heritage, visitors can contribute to its preservation.

Supporting Local Communities:

Sustainable tourism aims to benefit local communities by promoting economic opportunities and empowering local businesses. Travelers can support the local economy by choosing locally owned accommodations, dining at locally owned restaurants, and purchasing products from local artisans and farmers. Engaging in community-based tourism initiatives, such as homestays and village tours, provides direct benefits to local families and encourages the preservation of traditional ways of life.

Responsible Wildlife Experiences:

Bali is home to a variety of unique wildlife, including endangered species such as sea turtles and Bali starlings. When engaging in wildlife experiences, it is essential to choose responsible operators that prioritize animal welfare and conservation. Avoid activities that involve animal exploitation or contribute to the illegal wildlife trade. Instead, opt for ethical encounters such as visiting animal sanctuaries or participating in conservation projects.

Sustainable Dining:

Bali's culinary scene is renowned for its flavors and variety. Sustainable dining in Bali involves supporting restaurants that prioritize local, seasonal, and organic ingredients. By choosing establishments that practice sustainable food sourcing and support local farmers, travelers can contribute to reducing the carbon footprint associated with food production and support sustainable agricultural practices.

Eco-Friendly Transportation:

Transportation plays a significant role in sustainable tourism. Opt for eco-friendly transportation options such as cycling, walking, or using public transportation whenever possible. When renting vehicles, choose fuel-efficient options and consider carpooling to reduce carbon emissions. Additionally, support initiatives that promote renewable energy and invest in eco-friendly infrastructure.

Engaging in Volunteering and Conservation Efforts:

For travelers who wish to make a more direct impact, volunteering with local conservation organizations can be a rewarding experience. There are numerous initiatives focused on environmental conservation, waste management, and community development. Engaging in these efforts allows travelers to contribute their time and skills to the sustainable development of Bali.

Educating and Spreading Awareness:

One of the most important aspects of sustainable tourism is educating oneself and others about responsible travel practices. By spreading awareness of sustainable tourism principles and sharing personal experiences, travelers can inspire others to make conscious choices that protect Bali's natural and cultural heritage.

In conclusion, sustainable tourism in Bali is about preserving the island's environment, culture, and communities for future generations to enjoy. By embracing responsible travel practices, travelers can minimize their ecological footprint, support local communities, and contribute to the overall well-being of Bali. Let us all play our part in creating a sustainable future for this remarkable destination.

Balinese Language and Basic Phrases

Immersing yourself in the local culture is an essential part of any travel experience, and learning a few basic phrases in the native language can go a long way in connecting with the local people and understanding their way of life. In Bali, the official language is Indonesian, but the Balinese people also speak their own unique language, Balinese. While English is widely spoken in tourist areas, making an effort to communicate in the local language shows respect and can enhance your interactions with the locals. In this chapter, we will introduce you to the Balinese language and provide you with some basic phrases to help you navigate your way through the island.

Greetings and Polite Expressions:

Good morning: Selamat pagi (suh-lah-maht pah-gee)

Good afternoon: Selamat siang (suh-lah-maht see-yahng)

Good evening: Selamat malam (suh-lah-maht mah-lahm)

Thank you: Suksma (sook-suh-mah)

You're welcome: Sampunang (sum-poo-nahng)

Excuse me: Matur suksma (mah-toor sook-suh-mah)

Sorry: Maaf (mah-ahf)

Basic Conversation:

What is your name?: Ngalan dane punapi?

(ngah-lahn dah-neh poo-nah-pee?)

My name is...: Nika ngalane... (nee-kah ngah-lah-neh...)

How are you?: Napi sane paling becik? (nah-pee sah-neh pah-leeng beh-cheek?)

I'm fine, thank you: Tiang becik, suksma (tee-ahng beh-cheek, sook-suh-mah)

Where is...?: Dumun ring...? (doo-moon reeng...?)

I don't understand: Tiang tusing ngerti (tee-ahng too-sing ngair-tee)

Do you speak English?: Kakang mawinan ngawangun basa Inggris? (kah-kahng mah-wee-nahn ngah-wahng-oon bah-sah ing-gris?)

Directions and Transportation:

Where is the toilet?: Pupuksane dumun ring pamedekan? (poo-pook-sah-neh doo-moon reeng pah-meh-deh-kahn?)

How much does it cost?: Mapinunan ring dewek? (mah-pee-noo-nahn reeng deh-wek?)

Left: Kiri (kee-ree)

Right: Kanan (kah-nahn)

Straight ahead: Lurus (loo-roos)

Taxi: Taksi (tahk-see)

How far is...?: Sampunang ring ngene mapinunan ring...? (sum-poo-nahng reeng ngay-neh mah-pee-noo-nahn reeng...?)

Food and Dining:

I would like...: Tiang ngelah... (tee-ahng ngay-lah...)

Water: Tirtha (teer-thah)

Rice: Nasi (nah-see)

Vegetables: Sayur-sayuran (sah-yoor-sah-yoor-ahn)

Delicious: Sedap (seh-dahp)

Bill, please: Mapinunan ring rasi, suksma (mah-pee-noo-nahn reeng rah-see, sook-suh-mah)

Shopping and Bargaining:

How much?: Mapinunan ring dewek? (mah-pee-noo-nahn reeng deh-wek?)

Expensive: Mahal (mah-hahl)

Cheap: Murah (moo-rah)

Can you lower the price?: Tusing ringin dek? (too-sing reeng-een dek?)

I will take it: Tiang maan (tee-ahng mah-ahn)

Numbers:

One: Siki (see-kee)

Two: Lian (lee-ahn)

Three: Telu (teh-loo)

Four: Papat (pah-paht)

Five: Lima (lee-mah)

Remember, learning a new language takes practice and patience. The Balinese people appreciate any effort you make to speak their language, no matter how basic. Don't be afraid to make mistakes and embrace the opportunity to learn from the locals. They will be delighted to see your enthusiasm in connecting with their culture. So, practice these phrases, engage with the Balinese people, and enjoy the warmth and friendliness that Bali has to offer.

Staying Safe and Healthy in Bali

Ensuring your safety and well-being is crucial when traveling to any destination, and Bali is no exception. While Bali is generally a safe place for tourists, it is essential to be aware of certain precautions and take necessary measures to stay safe and healthy during your visit. In this chapter, we will provide you with valuable tips and guidelines to help you have a safe and enjoyable experience in Bali.

Travel Insurance:

Before embarking on your trip to Bali, it is highly recommended to purchase comprehensive travel insurance that covers medical expenses, trip cancellation or interruption, and personal belongings. Having travel insurance will provide you with peace of mind and financial protection in case of any unforeseen circumstances.

Health Precautions:

a. Vaccinations: Ensure that you are up to date on routine vaccinations before traveling to Bali. Consult with your healthcare provider or a travel health clinic to receive recommended vaccinations, including hepatitis A and B, typhoid, tetanus, and measles.

b. Water and Food Safety: Drink only bottled water or water that has been properly treated and avoid consuming ice cubes in drinks. Be cautious when eating street food and choose reputable establishments to minimize the risk of foodborne illnesses. Wash your hands regularly with soap and water, or use hand sanitizers when necessary.

c. Mosquito-Borne Diseases: Bali is considered a low-risk area for diseases such as dengue fever and malaria, but it is still advisable to take precautions. Use insect repellent containing DEET, wear long-sleeved clothing and long pants, and consider staying in accommodations with proper mosquito control measures.

Sun Protection:

Bali's tropical climate means abundant sunshine year-round. Protect yourself from harmful UV rays by wearing sunscreen with a high SPF, a wide-brimmed hat, sunglasses, and lightweight clothing that covers your skin. Seek shade during the peak sun hours and stay hydrated by drinking plenty of water.

Traffic and Transportation:

a. Road Safety: Traffic in Bali can be congested, and road conditions may vary. Exercise caution when crossing the street and use designated pedestrian crossings whenever possible. If you plan to rent a motorbike or car, ensure that you have the necessary licenses and wear helmets for motorbike rides.

b. Hiring Drivers: If you hire a driver or use transportation services, choose licensed and reputable operators. Ensure that the vehicle is in good condition and that the driver adheres to traffic regulations. Avoid unlicensed taxis and use official taxi services or ride-hailing apps.

Personal Safety:

a. Valuables and Personal Belongings: Keep your valuables, including passports, cash, and electronic devices, secure and locked in a hotel safe when not in use. Be cautious of your surroundings and avoid displaying expensive jewelry or belongings that may attract unwanted attention.

b. Beach Safety: While Bali's beaches are beautiful, it's essential to practice beach safety. Observe warning flags and signs, swim in designated areas with lifeguards, and be cautious of strong currents and riptides. If you're not a strong swimmer, consider using a life jacket or staying in shallow waters.

Cultural Sensitivity:

a. Dress Respectfully: Bali is known for its rich culture and religious traditions. When visiting temples or religious sites, dress modestly and respectfully, covering your shoulders and knees. Respect local customs and traditions by dressing appropriately in public areas.

b. Etiquette: Be polite, courteous, and respectful to the Balinese people. Learn and use basic Balinese greetings and phrases, as this shows appreciation for their culture. Ask for permission before taking someone's photograph, especially during religious ceremonies or in private spaces.

Emergency Contacts:

Save important contact numbers, including the local police (110) and ambulance services (118), on your phone in case of emergencies. Familiarize yourself with the location of the nearest hospitals or clinics and keep a copy of your travel insurance information readily available.

Remember, these safety guidelines are meant to enhance your travel experience in Bali, not to discourage exploration or enjoyment. By taking these precautions, you can have a worry-free and memorable trip on the beautiful island of Bali. Enjoy your time, embrace the local culture, and create lasting memories while prioritizing your safety and well-being.

Accommodation Options in Bali: From Budget to Luxury

Finding the perfect place to stay is a vital part of planning any trip, and Bali offers a wide range of accommodation options to suit every budget and preference. Whether you're looking for a budget-friendly hostel, a comfortable mid-range hotel, or a luxurious beachfront resort, Bali has it all. In this chapter, we will explore the various accommodation options available in Bali, helping you make an informed decision that suits your needs and enhances your overall travel experience.

Budget Accommodation:

For budget-conscious travelers, Bali offers a multitude of affordable accommodation options, including guesthouses, homestays, and hostels. These establishments provide basic amenities and a cozy atmosphere, often allowing you to interact with fellow travelers. Budget accommodation can be found in popular tourist areas like Kuta, Seminyak, and Ubud, as well as in quieter regions for a more authentic local experience.

Mid-Range Hotels and Resorts:

If you're seeking a balance between comfort and affordability, Bali has a wide selection of mid-range hotels and resorts. These accommodations offer comfortable rooms, various facilities such as swimming pools, on-site restaurants, and often have convenient locations close to popular attractions. Seminyak, Nusa Dua, and Sanur are some areas known for their mid-range accommodation options.

Villas and Private Rentals:

For those looking for more privacy and a home-away-from-home experience, renting a villa or private accommodation can be an excellent choice. Bali boasts a vast array of villas in different locations, from secluded areas surrounded by lush rice fields to beachfront properties with stunning ocean views. Villas come in various sizes, ranging from cozy one-bedroom units to large properties suitable for families or groups of friends.

Boutique and Design Hotels:

Bali has seen an emergence of boutique and design hotels that offer a unique and stylish experience. These properties often feature creative architecture, trendy interiors, and personalized services. Staying in a boutique hotel allows you to immerse yourself in the local culture while enjoying a distinctive and memorable accommodation experience.

Luxury Resorts and Hotels:

For those seeking the ultimate indulgence, Bali is renowned for its luxury resorts and hotels that provide world-class amenities and impeccable service. From beachfront resorts in Seminyak to cliff-top retreats in Uluwatu, these properties offer exquisite accommodations, private pools, spa facilities, fine dining options, and breathtaking views. Some luxury resorts even have private villas with butler service, ensuring a truly unforgettable stay.

Eco-Friendly and Sustainable Accommodation:

Bali is also home to eco-friendly and sustainable accommodation options that promote responsible tourism. These establishments prioritize environmentally friendly practices, such as using renewable energy, minimizing waste, and supporting local communities. By choosing eco-friendly accommodation, you can enjoy your stay while minimizing your impact on the environment.

Unique and Alternative Accommodation:

In addition to traditional accommodation options, Bali offers unique and alternative choices for a more unconventional experience. You can find treehouses nestled in the jungle, bamboo cottages, or even traditional Balinese-style bungalows. These offbeat accommodations provide a distinctive stay and allow you to immerse yourself in the island's natural beauty.

When choosing your accommodation in Bali, consider factors such as location, amenities, budget, and the type of experience you desire. Research and read reviews from previous guests to gain insights into the quality and service provided. Booking in advance, particularly during peak seasons, is recommended to secure the best options.

Remember, Bali's charm extends beyond its accommodation options. The island offers a wealth of attractions and activities to explore, so choose an accommodation that serves as a comfortable base for your adventures. Whether you opt for budget-friendly or luxury accommodation, Bali's hospitality will ensure a memorable stay.

Navigating Bali's Transportation System

Bali, known as the "Island of the Gods," offers visitors a multitude of transportation options to explore its stunning landscapes, vibrant culture, and picturesque beaches. From taxis to motorbikes and traditional modes of transport, this chapter will guide you through Bali's transportation system, helping you navigate the island efficiently and make the most of your travel experience.

Taxis and Ride-Hailing Apps:

Taxis are a popular mode of transportation in Bali, providing a convenient way to get around. Official taxi companies such as Bluebird, Grab, and Gojek operate in Bali, and you can easily hail a taxi on the street or use a ride-hailing app to book a ride. Ensure that the taxi uses a meter or agree on a price before starting the journey. Be aware of unofficial taxis and negotiate the fare in advance to avoid any surprises.

Motorbike Rental:

Renting a motorbike is a popular choice among travelers in Bali, offering flexibility and the freedom to explore at your own pace. Many rental agencies provide motorbikes for daily or weekly use. Before renting, ensure that you have a valid international driving license and wear a helmet at all times. Familiarize yourself with local traffic rules and be cautious when driving, as Bali's roads can be busy and chaotic.

Car Rental:

If you prefer the comfort and convenience of a

car, renting a vehicle is a viable option in Bali. Numerous car rental companies operate on the island, offering a variety of vehicles to suit your needs. Ensure that you have a valid international driving license and familiarize yourself with Bali's traffic rules. Be prepared for heavy traffic in popular tourist areas and plan your routes accordingly.

Public Buses:

Bali's public bus system is limited compared to other modes of transportation. However, Trans Sarbagita buses operate in certain areas, providing an affordable option for traveling between major towns and attractions. The routes and schedules may be limited, so check the bus routes and timings in advance. Be prepared for crowded buses, especially during peak hours.

Bemo:

Bemo, also known as public minivans, are a traditional mode of transport in Bali. They follow specific routes and can be flagged down along the road. Bemo fares are generally lower than taxis, but they can be crowded and may not operate on fixed schedules. Bemos are a more adventurous and authentic way to experience local transportation in Bali.

Motorbike Taxis:

For short distances or navigating through traffic, motorbike taxis, known as ojeks, are a popular choice. Ojeks can be found near tourist areas, and you can negotiate the fare with the driver before starting the ride. Ensure that you wear a helmet and agree on the price in advance.

Traditional Transportation:

Bali is known for its traditional transportation methods, offering unique experiences for visitors. Take a ride on a dokar (horse-drawn carriage) in rural areas, or explore the scenic countryside on a bicycle. These traditional modes of transport allow you to immerse yourself in Bali's culture and enjoy a slower pace of travel.

Getting to and from the Airport:

Ngurah Rai International Airport, located near Denpasar, is Bali's main gateway. Various transportation options are available to transfer between the airport and your accommodation. Taxis, ride-hailing apps, and airport transfer services are readily available. Pre-arranging airport transfers with your hotel or booking a private driver in advance can ensure a smooth arrival and departure.

Tips for Navigating Bali's Transportation System:

Plan your routes and allow ample time for travel, especially during peak hours.

Carry small denominations of Indonesian Rupiah for payment, as drivers may not always have change for larger bills.

Be cautious of traffic and road conditions, particularly when driving a motorbike.

Use GPS or navigation apps to help you find your way around.

Consider hiring a private driver for longer distances or if you prefer not to drive yourself.

Stay alert and keep your belongings secure, especially in crowded areas or public transportation.

Remember, Bali's transportation system can be diverse and exciting, but it's important to prioritize your safety and choose reliable and reputable options. Whether you opt for taxis, motorbikes, or traditional modes of transport, exploring Bali's stunning landscapes and vibrant culture will be a memorable adventure. Enjoy the journey and embrace the island's unique transportation experiences.

Understanding Balinese Customs and Etiquette

When visiting Bali, it's essential to be mindful of the local customs and etiquette to show respect for the Balinese people and their rich cultural heritage. The Balinese are known for their warm hospitality and strong sense of community, and by familiarizing yourself with their customs, you can enhance your travel experience and create positive interactions. In this chapter, we will explore some key customs and etiquette practices to help you navigate Balinese culture with ease.

Greeting and Politeness:

Balinese people are friendly and polite, and it is customary to greet others with a smile and a warm "Om Swastiastu" (meaning "May peace be with you"). When entering temples or traditional compounds, it is polite to dress modestly, remove your shoes, and cover your shoulders. It's also customary to use your right hand for giving or receiving objects and when shaking hands or offering a gift.

Respect for the Balinese Religion:

Religion holds significant importance in Bali, with the majority of the population practicing Hinduism. Visitors should respect the Balinese religious customs and ceremonies. When visiting temples, follow the dress code and guidelines provided. Observe and participate respectfully in rituals, and avoid pointing your feet towards the shrines or stepping on offerings placed on the ground.

Balinese Temples and Sacred Sites:

Bali is home to numerous temples and sacred sites, and they are an integral part of the island's cultural identity. When visiting these places, it's crucial to show respect. Dress modestly, cover your shoulders and knees, and wear a sarong and sash if required. Keep your voice low, avoid touching the sacred objects, and ask for permission before taking photographs, especially during ceremonies.

Balinese Offerings:

Offerings, known as "canang sari," are an essential part of daily life in Bali. These small baskets made of palm leaves are filled with flowers, rice, and other symbolic items. It is important to be mindful and not disturb or step on the offerings placed on the ground. If you encounter them, it is polite to walk around them rather than over them.

Balinese Social Hierarchy:

Balinese society has a social hierarchy based on age and status. It is customary to greet elders and people of higher status first and to use appropriate titles when addressing them. The use of "Bapak" for men and "Ibu" for women, followed by their first name, is a polite way to address someone.

Balinese Traditional Arts and Performances:

Bali is renowned for its traditional arts, including dance, music, and crafts. When watching performances or visiting art studios, show appreciation for the artists' skills and talent. It is customary to sit quietly during performances and refrain from talking or using flash photography, as it can disrupt the performers and other audience members.

Balinese Social Interactions:

The Balinese value harmonious relationships and community. It is polite to engage in small talk and show interest in the local culture when interacting with the Balinese. Take the time to learn a few basic phrases in the Balinese language, such as "Suksma" (thank you) and "Matur Suksma" (thank you very much), as it will be greatly appreciated.

Environmental Awareness:

Bali's natural beauty is a significant attraction for visitors. It's important to be mindful of the environment and practice responsible tourism. Dispose of waste properly, avoid littering, and support eco-friendly initiatives. Respect the natural habitats, wildlife, and marine life by refraining from touching or disturbing them.

By embracing these customs and etiquette practices, you can foster positive interactions with the Balinese people and gain a deeper understanding of their culture. Remember, showing respect and appreciation for their customs will not only enhance your travel experience but also contribute to the preservation of Bali's unique heritage for generations to come.

Volunteer and Community Engagement Opportunities in Bali

While exploring the breathtaking landscapes and rich cultural heritage of Bali, many travelers find themselves inspired to give back to the local community. Bali offers a range of volunteer and community engagement opportunities that allow visitors to make a positive impact during their stay. This chapter will guide you through some of the meaningful ways you can get involved and contribute to the well-being of the Balinese people and the island as a whole.

Education and Teaching Programs:

Education is a vital area where volunteers can make a significant difference in Bali. Many organizations and schools welcome volunteers to support teaching English, computer skills, or other subjects. By sharing your knowledge and skills, you can empower local children and contribute to their educational development. These programs often provide a unique opportunity to exchange cultural experiences and create lasting connections with the Balinese community.

Environmental Conservation:

Bali's natural beauty is a treasure that needs to be preserved for future generations. Numerous conservation organizations and projects are dedicated to protecting the island's ecosystems and marine life. Volunteers can participate in activities such as coral reef restoration, beach cleanups, reforestation projects, and wildlife conservation efforts. These initiatives provide an opportunity to learn about environmental issues, contribute to conservation efforts, and raise awareness about sustainable practices.

Community Development:

Bali is home to many local communities that can benefit from volunteer support in various areas of development. You can engage in projects focused on infrastructure improvement, access to clean water, sanitation, healthcare, or economic empowerment. By working directly with local communities, you can make a tangible impact on their living conditions and enhance their quality of life.

Animal Welfare:

Animal rescue and conservation organizations in Bali offer volunteer opportunities for those passionate about animal welfare. You can assist in caring for rescued animals, rehabilitation programs, or working on projects aimed at reducing animal exploitation and promoting responsible tourism practices. These initiatives provide a chance to contribute to the well-being of animals and promote ethical treatment.

Women's Empowerment:

Several initiatives in Bali focus on empowering women and supporting gender equality. Volunteering with organizations that provide vocational training, entrepreneurship support, or educational opportunities for women can help create economic independence and improve their overall well-being. By engaging in these programs, you can contribute to the empowerment and social advancement of Balinese women.

Health and Medical Programs:

Medical and healthcare volunteer programs are available in Bali, allowing you to assist local healthcare professionals, clinics, or hospitals. This involvement can range from providing basic healthcare services to participating in public health education campaigns. Such programs are an excellent opportunity to share your medical expertise, promote health awareness, and make a positive impact on the local community's well-being.

Sustainable Farming and Permaculture:

Bali's fertile lands provide an ideal environment for sustainable farming and permaculture practices. Volunteers can participate in projects that promote organic farming, agroforestry, or permaculture techniques. These initiatives aim to improve food security, promote sustainable agriculture, and preserve traditional farming methods. You can learn about Balinese agricultural practices and actively contribute to sustainable food production.

Voluntourism Programs:

Voluntourism combines volunteering with travel experiences, allowing you to engage in meaningful activities while exploring Bali's attractions. These programs often include a combination of volunteer work, cultural immersion, and guided tours. While choosing voluntourism, ensure that the programs have a responsible and sustainable approach and prioritize local community needs.

When considering volunteer opportunities in Bali, it's crucial to choose reputable organizations that have a positive track record and align with your values. Here are some tips to keep in mind:

Research organizations and projects thoroughly before committing to ensure they are reputable and transparent about their impact.

Understand the expectations and requirements of the volunteer program, including the duration, costs (if any), and the skills or qualifications needed.

Respect the local culture and customs, and be open to learning from the Balinese community.

Prioritize ethical practices and avoid activities that exploit vulnerable populations or harm the environment.

Consider the long-term sustainability of the volunteer project and its impact on the local community.

Volunteering and engaging with the community in Bali can be a rewarding and transformative experience. It allows you to create meaningful connections, gain a deeper understanding of Balinese culture, and contribute to the island's sustainable development. By dedicating your time and skills to the causes that matter to you, you can leave a positive and lasting impact on Bali and its people.

Exploring Bali's Hidden Gems

While Bali is known for its stunning beaches, vibrant culture, and iconic attractions, there is a wealth of hidden gems waiting to be discovered by intrepid travelers. These lesser-known destinations offer a chance to escape the crowds and delve into the island's natural beauty, tranquil landscapes, and unique cultural experiences. In this chapter, we will uncover some of Bali's hidden gems that will leave you awe-inspired and longing to explore more.

Sidemen Valley:

Tucked away in the eastern part of Bali, Sidemen Valley is a picturesque region characterized by lush green rice terraces, winding rivers, and traditional villages. This hidden gem offers a serene escape from the bustling tourist areas. Take a leisurely stroll through the emerald-green rice fields, interact with friendly locals, and immerse yourself in the traditional Balinese way of life. Don't miss the opportunity to witness mesmerizing sunrise views from the vantage points in Sidemen Valley.

Nusa Penida:

Located just off the coast of Bali, Nusa Penida is a paradise for nature enthusiasts and adventurers. This island is renowned for its dramatic cliffs, crystal-clear turquoise waters, and pristine white-sand beaches. Explore hidden coves and secret beaches, such as Atuh Beach and Crystal Bay. Marvel at natural wonders like

Kelingking Beach, known for its T-Rex-shaped cliff, and the awe-inspiring Angel's Billabong and Broken Beach. Nusa Penida offers a rugged and untouched charm that will captivate your senses.

Jatiluwih Rice Terraces:

For a truly mesmerizing experience, head to the Jatiluwih Rice Terraces in central Bali. This UNESCO World Heritage site boasts expansive terraced rice fields set against a backdrop of majestic Mount Batukaru. Take a leisurely hike or rent a bicycle to explore the picturesque landscapes, and witness the traditional farming methods that have been practiced for centuries. The Jatiluwih Rice Terraces offer a glimpse into Bali's agricultural heritage and provide a tranquil retreat away from the tourist crowds.

Tirta Gangga:

Located in East Bali, Tirta Gangga is a serene water palace renowned for its beautiful gardens, fountains, and sacred pools. Built by the royal family of Karangasem, this enchanting retreat is adorned with intricate stone carvings and statues. Take a leisurely stroll through the lush gardens, cross ornate stepping stones over the lotus ponds, and rejuvenate your senses by dipping into the natural spring water pools. Tirta Gangga offers a peaceful and enchanting ambiance, perfect for relaxation and reflection.

Menjangan Island:

If you're a fan of snorkeling or diving, Menjangan Island in West Bali is a hidden gem waiting to be explored. This small island is part of the West Bali National Park and boasts pristine coral reefs, abundant marine life, and crystal-clear waters. Dive into the vibrant underwater world, where you can spot colorful coral gardens, turtles, and a variety of tropical fish. Menjangan Island offers a tranquil escape for nature lovers and underwater enthusiasts.

Amed:

Escape the tourist crowds and head to the tranquil coastal village of Amed, located on Bali's northeast coast. This hidden gem is known for its black volcanic sand beaches, vibrant coral reefs, and excellent snorkeling and diving opportunities. Explore the underwater wonders, go on a traditional fishing boat ride, or simply relax on the peaceful shores. Amed provides a serene and laid-back atmosphere, making it an ideal spot to unwind and connect with Bali's natural beauty.

Blahmantung Waterfall:

Located in the central highlands of Bali, Blahmantung Waterfall is a hidden gem that offers a refreshing and adventurous experience. Trek through lush forests, cross bamboo bridges, and be rewarded with the sight of a cascading waterfall nestled amidst the tranquil surroundings. Take a dip in the natural pool or simply enjoy the serenity of the area while listening to the soothing sounds of nature. Blahmantung Waterfall is a true hidden gem for nature lovers and outdoor enthusiasts.

Tenganan Village:

For a glimpse into Bali's ancient traditions and cultural heritage, visit Tenganan Village in East Bali. This secluded village is home to the Bali Aga people, who have preserved their unique customs and rituals for centuries. Explore the traditional architecture, intricate handwoven textiles, and ancient rituals that are still practiced today. Tenganan Village offers a fascinating insight into Bali's rich cultural tapestry and provides an opportunity to connect with the local community.

As you venture off the beaten path and discover Bali's hidden gems, remember to be respectful of the local communities and the natural environment. Embrace the sense of adventure and allow yourself to be captivated by the lesser-known wonders that Bali has to offer. These hidden gems will create memories that will stay with you long after your journey comes to an end.

Outdoor Activities and Adventure Sports in Bali

Bali is not only a paradise for beach lovers and culture enthusiasts but also a haven for outdoor adventurers seeking thrilling experiences and adrenaline-pumping activities. From water sports to trekking, Bali offers a wide range of outdoor activities and adventure sports that cater to all levels of thrill-seekers. In this chapter, we will explore some of the top outdoor activities and adventure sports that will get your heart racing and create unforgettable memories.

Surfing:

Bali's world-class waves and consistent surf breaks have made it a mecca for surfers from around the globe. Whether you're a beginner or an experienced surfer, there are surf spots suitable for all levels. Kuta Beach, Uluwatu, and Canggu are popular surf destinations offering a variety of breaks. Take a surf lesson, rent a board, and ride the waves under the guidance of experienced instructors. Surfing in Bali is an exhilarating experience that should not be missed.

White Water Rafting:

Embark on a thrilling white water rafting adventure on Bali's pristine rivers. The Ayung River and Telaga Waja River are popular spots for rafting, offering a combination of adrenaline-pumping rapids and stunning natural scenery. Paddle through cascading waterfalls, lush rainforests, and steep canyons as you navigate the river's twists and turns. White water rafting is a fantastic way to experience Bali's wild side and enjoy a dose of adventure.

Scuba Diving and Snorkeling:

Bali's crystal-clear waters and vibrant marine life make it a haven for scuba diving and snorkeling enthusiasts. Explore the colorful coral reefs, encounter tropical fish, and discover underwater treasures. Tulamben, Amed, and Menjangan Island are popular dive sites offering excellent visibility and diverse marine ecosystems. Whether you're a certified diver or a beginner looking to try a Discover Scuba Diving program, Bali's underwater world is sure to leave you in awe.

Jungle Trekking and Hiking:

Bali's lush jungles and scenic landscapes provide the perfect backdrop for jungle trekking and hiking adventures. Mount Batur and Mount Agung are popular hiking destinations, offering stunning sunrise views and challenging trails. Explore the breathtaking beauty of Bali's rainforests, encounter exotic wildlife, and immerse yourself in the tranquility of nature. Guided tours are available to ensure a safe and enjoyable hiking experience.

Canyoning:

For the ultimate adventure experience, try canyoning in Bali's rugged canyons. Traverse through natural water slides, rappel down waterfalls, and jump into crystal-clear pools.

Canyoning tours typically include a combination of hiking, swimming, climbing, and abseiling, providing a thrilling and immersive adventure in the heart of Bali's wilderness.

ATV and Quad Biking:

Explore Bali's scenic landscapes and off-road trails on an ATV or quad bike adventure. Zoom through rice fields, muddy tracks, and jungle trails as you enjoy the thrill of off-road riding. Whether you choose a guided tour or go for a self-guided exploration, ATV and quad biking offer an exciting way to discover Bali's hidden gems and rural countryside.

Parasailing and Jet Skiing:

For water sports enthusiasts, Bali offers a range of thrilling activities such as parasailing and jet skiing. Soar above the turquoise waters while parasailing, enjoying breathtaking aerial views of the coastline. Take control of a jet ski and feel the rush as you speed across the waves. These activities are readily available at popular beach destinations like Nusa Dua, Tanjung Benoa, and Sanur.

Skydiving:

For the ultimate adrenaline rush, experience the thrill of skydiving over Bali's picturesque landscapes. Jump from a plane at thousands of feet above the ground and freefall before your parachute opens, offering a bird's-eye view of Bali's stunning beauty. Tandem skydiving options are available for beginners, allowing you to enjoy this extreme sport under the guidance of experienced instructors.

As you embark on your outdoor adventures and engage in adventure sports in Bali, it's essential to prioritize safety. Choose reputable operators that prioritize safety measures, provide quality equipment, and have experienced guides. Always follow the instructions and guidelines given by the professionals to ensure a safe and enjoyable experience.

Bali's outdoor activities and adventure sports offer a thrilling escape from the ordinary, allowing you to immerse yourself in the island's natural wonders and embrace your adventurous spirit. Whether you're seeking the rush of riding the waves, the excitement of exploring underwater worlds, or the exhilaration of conquering challenging trails, Bali has it all for outdoor enthusiasts. So gear up, get ready to push your limits, and create unforgettable memories in Bali's outdoor playground.

Planning a Romantic Getaway in Bali

Bali's enchanting landscapes, stunning beaches, and vibrant culture make it an ideal destination for a romantic getaway. Whether you're celebrating your honeymoon, an anniversary, or simply looking to spend quality time with your loved one, Bali offers a plethora of romantic experiences and idyllic settings. In this chapter, we will guide you through planning a memorable and romantic escape in Bali.

Choosing the Perfect Accommodation:

Start your romantic getaway by selecting the perfect accommodation that sets the mood for romance. Bali offers a range of luxurious resorts, boutique hotels, and private villas that cater to couples seeking privacy and indulgence. Consider staying in secluded resorts with breathtaking views, private pools, and intimate settings to create a romantic atmosphere.

Romantic Beaches:

Bali is renowned for its pristine beaches, and there's nothing more romantic than a stroll hand-in-hand along the shore, watching the sunset paint the sky with vibrant hues. Head to Seminyak Beach, Nusa Dua Beach, or Jimbaran Beach for a romantic beach experience. Book a beachfront table at a cozy restaurant and enjoy a candlelit dinner while listening to the soothing sound of the waves.

Sunset Cruises:

Indulge in a romantic sunset cruise and set sail

along Bali's coastline as the sun dips below the horizon. These cruises offer a romantic ambiance, complete with onboard dining, live music, and breathtaking views. Raise a glass of champagne with your loved one as you toast to the beauty of the moment and create memories that will last a lifetime.

Couples' Spa Retreats:

Pamper yourselves with a couples' spa retreat in one of Bali's world-class spas. Indulge in relaxing massages, soothing treatments, and rejuvenating therapies, all designed to enhance your sense of well-being and create an intimate experience. Bali's spas offer serene settings and luxurious facilities, ensuring that you and your partner feel completely relaxed and rejuvenated.

Romantic Dinners:

Bali boasts a vibrant culinary scene, and there are plenty of options for romantic dinners. From candlelit beachfront dinners to private dining in lush gardens, you can choose from a variety of romantic settings. Book a table at a fine-dining restaurant serving delectable cuisine, or opt for a more intimate experience with a private chef preparing a personalized meal in your villa.

Balinese Cultural Experiences:

Immerse yourselves in Bali's rich culture and create lasting memories with unique cultural experiences. Attend a traditional Balinese dance performance, visit local temples, or participate in a purification ritual at a sacred water temple. These cultural encounters will deepen your connection with the island and provide a glimpse into the Balinese way of life.

Private Excursions:

Escape the crowds and embark on private excursions to explore Bali's hidden gems with your loved one. Hire a private guide and driver to take you to lesser-known destinations such as hidden waterfalls, secluded beaches, or picturesque rice terraces. This allows you to create intimate moments in breathtaking settings and enjoy the beauty of Bali's natural landscapes together.

Romantic Adventures:

For adventurous couples, Bali offers a range of activities that combine excitement and romance. Go on a sunrise trek up Mount Batur and witness the breathtaking views from the summit. Take a thrilling ATV ride through rice fields and jungles, or go on a tandem paragliding adventure and soar above the island's scenic landscapes. These adrenaline-pumping activities will ignite your sense of adventure and create shared experiences.

Romantic Walks in Ubud:

Ubud, Bali's cultural heart, provides a serene and picturesque setting for romantic walks. Stroll through the lush Monkey Forest, visit the beautiful Tegalalang Rice Terrace, or explore the vibrant Ubud Art Market hand-in-hand with your loved one. Ubud's serene ambiance and artistic charm make it a perfect destination for couples seeking a romantic escape.

Private Yoga or Meditation Sessions:

Deepen your connection with your partner and find inner peace together with private yoga or meditation sessions. Bali's tranquil settings and spiritual energy make it an ideal place to practice yoga or meditation. Whether you're beginners or experienced practitioners, there are experienced instructors who can guide you through a personalized session that nourishes your mind, body, and soul.

When planning your romantic getaway in Bali, it's important to consider your partner's preferences and interests. Tailor the itinerary to create a personalized experience that reflects your shared passions and desires. Whether you're indulging in luxury, exploring nature, or immersing yourselves in the local culture, Bali offers a romantic escape that will ignite the flame of love and create cherished memories that will last a lifetime.

Exploring Bali's Art and Design Scene

Bali's vibrant and diverse art scene has long been a draw for creative minds from around the world. From traditional Balinese arts and crafts to contemporary galleries and design studios, the island is a treasure trove of artistic expression. In this chapter, we will delve into the rich art and design scene of Bali, showcasing its unique cultural heritage and creative spirit.

Traditional Balinese Arts:

Immerse yourself in the rich traditions of Balinese art by exploring its various forms. Traditional Balinese painting, known as Kamasan or Ubud style, is characterized by intricate detailing, vibrant colors, and mythological themes. Visit the villages of Ubud, Batuan, and Mas to witness artists at work and discover their masterpieces.

Balinese Woodcarving:

Bali is renowned for its intricate woodcarvings, which depict religious and mythological figures, as well as everyday scenes. The village of Mas is a hub for woodcarving, where you can witness skilled artisans chiseling elaborate designs out of locally sourced wood. You can even try your hand at woodcarving by joining a workshop and create your own unique piece of art.

Batik and Textiles:

Bali's textile industry is known for its exquisite batik and handwoven fabrics. Batik is a traditional art form where intricate designs are created using wax-resist dyeing techniques. Explore the markets of Ubud and Sanur to find beautiful batik pieces, ranging from clothing and scarves to home decor items. Additionally, the village of Sidemen is renowned for its traditional ikat weaving, where intricate patterns are created by tying and dyeing the threads before they are woven.

Contemporary Art Galleries:

Bali is home to a thriving contemporary art scene, with numerous galleries showcasing the works of local and international artists. Seminyak, Ubud, and Canggu are popular areas where you can find a plethora of galleries, each with its own unique style and artistic expression. Take a leisurely stroll through the galleries, admire the diverse artworks, and even purchase a piece to bring home as a lasting memento of your time in Bali.

Design Studios and Boutiques:

Bali's creative energy extends beyond traditional arts and into contemporary design. Explore the design studios and boutiques scattered across the island to discover unique furniture, home decor, and fashion items. The town of Kerobokan is known for its eclectic mix of design shops, where you can find one-of-a-kind pieces that blend modern aesthetics with traditional craftsmanship.

Art Markets and Artisan Villages:

For a more immersive experience, visit Bali's bustling art markets and artisan villages. The Ubud Art Market is a popular destination, offering a wide array of handicrafts, paintings, and souvenirs. The villages of Celuk and Sukawati are known for their silver and gold jewelry, where skilled artisans create intricate pieces using traditional techniques. Explore these markets and villages to support local artists and artisans while indulging in a unique shopping experience.

Art Workshops and Classes:

Unleash your own creativity by participating in art workshops and classes offered by local artists. Learn traditional painting techniques, try your hand at batik, or experiment with ceramics and pottery. These workshops provide a hands-on experience, allowing you to learn from talented artists and create your own unique artwork.

Art and Design Festivals:

Bali hosts various art and design festivals throughout the year, celebrating the island's creative spirit. The Ubud Writers & Readers Festival, Bali Arts Festival, and Sanur Village Festival are just a few examples of events that showcase a wide range of artistic disciplines, including literature, visual arts, music, and dance. Attending these festivals allows you to immerse yourself in the vibrant cultural scene of Bali and witness the works of both established and emerging artists.

Artisanal Crafts and Souvenirs:

Support local artisans and take home a piece of Bali's artistic heritage by purchasing artisanal crafts and souvenirs. From handcrafted ceramics and batik clothing to intricately carved masks and traditional musical instruments, you'll find a wide array of unique items that reflect Bali's artistic traditions.

Bali's art and design scene is a testament to the island's rich cultural heritage and creative spirit. Whether you're a seasoned art enthusiast or simply appreciate the beauty of artistic expression, exploring Bali's art galleries, design studios, and artisanal villages will provide you with a deeper appreciation for the island's cultural legacy. So take your time, immerse yourself in the vibrant world of Balinese art, and let your senses be inspired by the creative energy that permeates the island.

Yoga and Meditation Retreats in Bali

Bali has long been renowned as a haven for spiritual seekers, offering a tranquil and picturesque setting for yoga and meditation retreats. With its lush landscapes, serene beaches, and vibrant spiritual culture, the island provides the perfect backdrop for individuals looking to deepen their practice, relax their minds, and rejuvenate their bodies. In this chapter, we will explore the world of yoga and meditation retreats in Bali, highlighting the various options available and the benefits they offer.

Ubud: The Yoga Hub of Bali:

Ubud, often referred to as the cultural heart of Bali, is a hotspot for yoga and meditation retreats. The town is home to numerous yoga studios, wellness centers, and retreat facilities, offering a wide range of programs to suit different preferences and levels of experience. Ubud's tranquil surroundings, lush rice fields, and spiritual energy make it an ideal destination for those seeking a deeper connection with themselves and their practice.

Retreat Centers and Resorts:

Bali boasts a plethora of retreat centers and resorts that specialize in yoga and meditation experiences. These centers provide comprehensive programs that combine daily yoga and meditation sessions, workshops, healing therapies, and nutritious organic meals. Some popular retreat centers include The Yoga Barn, Bali Spirit, and

Fivelements Retreat Bali. These centers offer a serene environment, experienced instructors, and a supportive community to enhance your retreat experience.

Beachside Retreats:

For those who prefer the soothing sounds of the ocean, Bali's coastal areas offer beachside retreats that allow you to immerse yourself in the elements of nature. Locations like Canggu, Seminyak, and Nusa Dua have retreat centers and resorts with yoga shalas overlooking the sea, providing a tranquil atmosphere for your practice. Start your day with a sunrise yoga session on the beach, followed by meditation to the sound of crashing waves.

Silent Retreats:

Bali also offers silent retreats, providing a unique opportunity to disconnect from the noise of everyday life and go inward. These retreats encourage participants to observe silence, practice mindfulness, and cultivate a deeper sense of self-awareness. Silent retreats often incorporate meditation, yoga, journaling, and nature walks, allowing you to delve into a profound state of introspection and personal growth.

Specialized Retreats and Workshops:

In addition to traditional yoga and meditation retreats, Bali hosts a variety of specialized retreats and workshops catering to specific interests and practices. These include Kundalini yoga retreats, Yin yoga retreats, Ayurveda retreats, and sound healing retreats, among others. These specialized programs offer a unique focus and provide an opportunity to delve deeper into a specific aspect of your practice.

Balinese Healing and Wellness:

Bali's spiritual culture is deeply rooted in ancient healing traditions, and many retreats incorporate Balinese healing therapies into their programs. These therapies, such as Balinese massage, traditional healing ceremonies, and energy work, complement the yoga and meditation practices, promoting holistic well-being and rejuvenation.

Nature Retreats and Eco-Lodges:

For those who seek a deeper connection with nature, Bali's nature retreats and eco-lodges offer a unique experience. These retreats are nestled in the island's lush jungles or amidst rice terraces, providing a serene and secluded environment. Engage in yoga and meditation surrounded by the sounds of nature, take nature walks, or participate in eco-conscious activities to foster a sense of harmony with the natural world.

Yoga Teacher Training:

Bali is a popular destination for yoga teacher training programs, attracting aspiring yoga teachers from around the globe. These intensive courses offer a comprehensive curriculum that covers yoga philosophy, asana practice, teaching methodology, and more. Bali's supportive and nurturing environment, combined with experienced teacher trainers, creates an ideal setting for embarking on your yoga teaching journey.

Retreats for All Levels:

Whether you're a beginner or an experienced practitioner, Bali's yoga and meditation retreats cater to all levels. Retreats often offer different class options and modifications, allowing participants to tailor their practice to their individual needs and abilities. This inclusivity makes Bali an inviting destination for anyone seeking to explore and deepen their practice.

Cultural Immersion:

In addition to yoga and meditation, Bali offers an immersive cultural experience. Many retreats incorporate visits to sacred temples, traditional ceremonies, and cultural activities, allowing participants to connect with the rich Balinese heritage and spiritual traditions. This cultural immersion adds a unique dimension to your retreat experience and offers a deeper understanding of the local culture.

Attending a yoga and meditation retreat in Bali provides a transformative experience that nourishes the body, mind, and soul. Whether you're seeking relaxation, self-reflection, spiritual growth, or simply a break from the demands of daily life, Bali's retreat offerings are designed to support and enhance your well-being. So take a step back, breathe deeply, and allow the enchanting island of Bali to guide you on a journey of self-discovery and inner peace.

Tips for Traveling with Kids in Bali

Traveling with kids can be a wonderful experience, and Bali offers a plethora of family-friendly activities and attractions that will keep children of all ages entertained. From stunning beaches to cultural experiences, the island has something for everyone. In this chapter, we will explore some helpful tips to ensure a smooth and enjoyable family vacation in Bali.

Plan Child-Friendly Activities:

Before traveling to Bali, research and plan activities that are suitable for children. Look for attractions such as water parks, animal encounters, interactive museums, and adventure parks. Popular destinations for kids include Waterbom Bali, Bali Safari and Marine Park, and the Bali Treetop Adventure Park. These attractions provide fun-filled experiences that will keep children engaged and entertained.

Choose Family-Friendly Accommodation:

Selecting the right accommodation is crucial when traveling with kids. Look for resorts or hotels that offer family-friendly amenities such as swimming pools, children's clubs, playgrounds, and spacious rooms or villas. Some accommodations even provide babysitting services, allowing parents to enjoy some time alone. Consider staying in areas like Nusa Dua, Sanur, or Seminyak, which are known for their family-friendly facilities and calm beaches.

Pack Essentials:

Pack essential items for your children, including sunscreen, insect repellent, hats, swimwear, and comfortable walking shoes. Bali's tropical climate requires protection from the sun and insects, and comfortable shoes are important for exploring the island. It's also a good idea to carry a small medical kit with basic medications and first aid supplies for any minor injuries or illnesses that may occur.

Be Mindful of Hygiene and Food Safety:

While Bali offers a wide range of dining options, it's important to be cautious about food safety when traveling with children. Stick to reputable restaurants and eateries that maintain high hygiene standards. Avoid street food or uncooked foods that may pose a risk of contamination. Ensure that your children wash their hands regularly, and carry hand sanitizers or wet wipes for added hygiene.

Take Precautions in the Sun:

Bali's tropical climate means exposure to strong sunlight. Protect your children from sunburn by applying sunscreen with a high SPF, dressing them in lightweight, long-sleeved clothing, and providing them with hats and sunglasses. Plan outdoor activities during the cooler parts of the day and seek shade when necessary. Hydration is also key, so encourage your children to drink plenty of water to stay hydrated.

Embrace Water Activities:

Bali is known for its beautiful beaches and water-based activities, which children often love. However, always prioritize safety when participating in water activities. Choose beaches with calm waters and lifeguards on duty. If you plan to engage in water sports, ensure that they are age-appropriate and that the necessary safety measures are in place. Consider enrolling your children in swimming lessons prior to the trip, so they can enjoy the water with confidence.

Discover Bali's Cultural Heritage:

Bali's rich cultural heritage provides a unique learning experience for children. Take them to visit traditional Balinese temples, where they can observe religious rituals and learn about the local customs and beliefs. Attend cultural performances, such as Balinese dance shows or gamelan music performances, which will captivate their imagination. Encourage them to try traditional Balinese crafts, such as batik painting or making traditional offerings.

Stay Flexible and Pace Yourself:

Traveling with children requires flexibility and understanding that their needs and energy levels may be different from adults. Allow for downtime and rest periods between activities to avoid overtiring them. Pace your itinerary accordingly, leaving room for spontaneous adventures or changes in plans. Flexibility will ensure a more enjoyable experience for everyone.

Engage in Nature and Wildlife Experiences:

Bali is home to diverse natural landscapes and wildlife. Take your children to explore the island's lush rice terraces, visit monkey forests, or go on nature walks in the countryside. Educational visits to butterfly parks, bird sanctuaries, or elephant conservation centers can be both fun and educational, providing children with the opportunity to learn about the environment and animal conservation.

Embrace the Balinese Warmth and Hospitality:

Balinese people are known for their friendliness and love for children. Embrace the warm and welcoming nature of the locals, who are often eager to interact with children. Encourage your children to learn a few basic Balinese phrases, as the locals will appreciate the effort and it can enhance their cultural experience.

Traveling with kids in Bali can be a rewarding experience filled with adventures, cultural discoveries, and family bonding. By following these tips and incorporating child-friendly activities into your itinerary, you can create lasting memories and ensure a memorable vacation for the whole family.

Saying Goodbye to Bali: Reflections and Memories

As your time in Bali comes to an end, it's natural to feel a mix of emotions. The island's enchanting beauty, warm hospitality, and vibrant culture leave a lasting impression on visitors. In this final chapter, we will reflect on the experiences and memories created during your journey through Bali, and offer some suggestions on how to make the most of your farewell to this remarkable destination.

Take a Moment of Reflection:

Before bidding farewell to Bali, find a quiet spot to reflect on your experiences. Whether it's sitting on a serene beach, overlooking the rice terraces, or meditating in a tranquil temple, take a moment to appreciate the beauty and tranquility that surrounded you during your stay. Allow yourself to savor the memories and reflect on how Bali has touched your heart and enriched your life.

Capture Your Memories:

Preserve your memories of Bali by capturing them through photographs, videos, or journal entries. Take time to revisit your favorite moments and relive the magic of the island. Whether it's the breathtaking sunsets, vibrant ceremonies, or the smiles of the Balinese people, these captured memories will serve as a reminder of the beauty and uniqueness of your Bali experience.

Connect with the Local Community:

Before leaving Bali, consider engaging with

the local community in a meaningful way. Participate in a cultural workshop, such as traditional dance or cooking classes, to deepen your understanding of Balinese customs and traditions. Visit local markets and interact with the artisans and craftsmen who create the island's unique arts and crafts. By connecting with the local community, you'll forge lasting connections and gain a deeper appreciation for the Balinese way of life.

Support Local Businesses:

As you prepare to say goodbye to Bali, show your appreciation for the local economy by supporting local businesses. Purchase souvenirs and handicrafts directly from local artisans, dine at locally-owned restaurants, and stay in boutique accommodations run by Balinese entrepreneurs. By supporting local businesses, you contribute to the sustainability and preservation of the island's unique culture and traditions.

Seek Closure in a Meaningful Way:

Consider engaging in a farewell ritual or ceremony to seek closure and express gratitude for your time in Bali. You may choose to participate in a traditional Balinese blessing or offer a small prayer at a temple as a gesture of respect and appreciation. These rituals can provide a sense of closure and allow you to say goodbye to Bali with a peaceful heart.

Embrace the Balinese Spirit:

One of the most profound aspects of Bali is its

spiritual essence. Take a moment to connect with your inner self and embrace the Balinese spirit of gratitude, mindfulness, and positivity. Carry these qualities with you as you bid farewell to the island, and strive to incorporate them into your daily life. Let the lessons you learned in Bali guide you on a path of personal growth and well-being.

Plan Your Return:

While saying goodbye to Bali may be bittersweet, it's comforting to know that the island will always be there, welcoming you back with open arms. Use your farewell as an opportunity to plan your return visit. Reflect on the experiences you missed or places you want to explore further, and start envisioning your next adventure in Bali. The anticipation of returning will keep the spirit of Bali alive within you.

Carry Bali with You:

Even as you leave Bali physically, carry the essence of the island with you in your heart and mind. Let the lessons learned, the moments cherished, and the beauty experienced shape your outlook on life. Embrace the kindness, serenity, and joy that Bali embodies, and infuse them into your daily routines. Bali has a way of leaving an indelible mark on its visitors, and by carrying its spirit, you can continue to nurture that connection wherever you go.

Saying goodbye to Bali is a poignant moment filled with gratitude, reflection, and a touch of nostalgia. It's a time to appreciate the transformative power of travel and the profound impact that a destination can have on our lives. As you bid farewell to Bali, remember that the memories, lessons, and connections made on the island will stay with you forever.

Printed by Libri Plureos GmbH in Hamburg, Germany